CHARLES COUNTY COMMUNITY COLLEGE

T5-DIJ-076

Blow Your Little Tin Whistle

A BIOGRAPHY OF RICHARD CLARKE SOMMERVILLE

Peggy A. Pittas

With three original essays by Richard C. Sommerville
Introduced and annotated by Elza C. Tiner

UNIVERSITY
PRESS OF
AMERICA

SCCCC - LIBRARY
4601 Mid Rivers Mall Drive
St. Peters, MO 63376

Lanham • New York • London

Copyright © 1992 by
University Press of America®, Inc.
4720 Boston Way
Lanham, Maryland 20706

3 Henrietta Street
London WC2E 8LU England

All rights reserved
Printed in the United States of America
British Cataloging in Publication Information Available

Library of Congress Cataloging-in-Publication Data

Pittas, Peggy A., 1944–
Blow your little tin whistle : a biography of Richard Clarke
Sommerville / by Peggy A. Pittas ; with three original essays by
Richard C. Sommerville ; introduced and annotated by Elza C. Tiner.
p.   cm.
Includes index.
1. Sommerville, Richard Clarke.   2. College teachers—
Virginia—Biography.   3. Lynchburg College.
I. Sommerville, Richard Clarke.   II. Tiner, Elza C.   III. Title.
LA2317.S636P58   1992
378.1'2'092—DC20   92–11142 CIP
[B]

ISBN 0–8191–8744–5 (cloth : alk. paper)
ISBN 0–8191–8745–3 (pbk. : alk. paper)

The paper used in this publication meets the minimum requirements of
American National Standard for Information Sciences—Permanence
of Paper for Printed Library Materials, ANSI Z39.48–1984.

To Totis—also a caring and excellent teacher

ACKNOWLEDGEMENTS

I am indebted to members of the Sommerville Family, especially to the late Dr. Felix B. Welton and to Mrs. Frances Welton of Black Mountain, North Carolina for opening their home and family records to me. They have stayed with the project, helping in every way possible.

I am especially indebted to and have come to appreciate archivists. Theirs is a fascinating career and they often work without recognition. I am grateful to Ms. Debra Beckel who for four years worked at Lynchburg College as the College Archivist and without whom this project would not have gotten off the ground; Mrs. Carol Pollack, Reference Librarian at Lynchburg College, who has the knack for directing anyone to just the right source to answer just about any question; Dr. Ruth See, Research Historian of the Historical Foundation of the Presbyterian and Reformed Churches, Inc., Montreat, North Carolina who spent many hours helping me locate information and for making me welcome at Montreat; Bonnie Greer, researcher, at the Arizona Historical Society, Flagstaff, Arizona, who spent countless hours researching the town records on my behalf; Dolores Swanson, Director of the Jones Memorial Library and a former student of Richard Sommerville, who helped not only with records from the Virginia Collection of the library, but who shared her insight and perspective of Dr. Sommerville; Margaret Hynds, Archivist, Austin College, Sherman, Texas for researching the Sommerville years of the Texas Presbyterian School for Girls; Lindsey P. Henderson, Jr., Col. AUS Ret., Fellow, Company of Military Historians, Historian, Georgia Hussars, for researching on

ACKNOWLEDGEMENTS

my behalf; Mr. Goodbar Morgan, Archivist of Southwestern at Memphis; and Capt. Thomas M. Weaver, Research Assistant/Librarian, Historical Society of the Militia and National Guard, Washington, D.C..

Others who have taken time to help and whose efforts are hereby acknowledged with gratitude include Mr. Paul R. Palmer, Curator, Columbia Collection, Columbia University; Ms. Ruby Hemphill, Supervisor of Transcripts and Inquiries, Office of Student Information, Columbia University; and James Huston, former dean of Lynchburg College, for his encouragement with this project.

I acknowledge with gratitude the following former students and colleagues who shared their memories and insights: Mrs. Belle Hill, Dr. Harold Garretson (deceased), Mr. Sam Gamble, Rev. Gordan Mason (deceased), Mr. William Shackelford, Mr. Stanley Jordan, Mr. Lavelon Sydnor, Mr. Malcolm Sydnor, Dr. William Dunn, Dr. Robert Hailey, Rev. Allan Stanger, Dr. Stuart Bruchey, Dr. John Turner, Dr. Fred Helsabeck, Dr. Joseph Smith, Mrs. Lorraine Flint, Mrs. Julia Hunter, Prof. Ruskin Freer (deceased), Dr. Carey Brewer, Dr. Joseph Nelson, Mr. and Mrs. George Adams, Mr. Don Evans, Mrs. Lucy Wilkins, Mrs. Charles Gilliland, Rev. Meredith Norment, Dr. Walter Wineman and Dr. Webb Fergusen.

I thank Dean James Traer of Lynchburg College for not only reading an early manuscript, but also for his constant support in helping to see the manuscript in print. I am also indebted to the Committee for Faculty Research and Development for helping to defray a portion of the expenses.

I am especially indebted to Ms. Virginia Redd,

ACKNOWLEDGEMENTS

retired Director of Development, to Professor John Brinkley, chairman of the Department of Classics, and to the librarians of Hampden-Sydney College, all of whom have spent many hours helping me with this endeavor, making me comfortable and extending to me every hospitality of that fine school.

I am truly grateful to Tracey Powell for her diligence in proofing parts of the manuscript.

My greatest debt is owed to Dr. Elza Tiner, who not only is a co-contributor to the book, but she has also spent countless hours editing the final manuscript. Elza is a truly remarkable and capable teacher who tirelessly works not only with her students, but also with her colleagues. Through her boundless energy, unfailing optimism, and love of teaching, she is an excellent model for both students and colleagues.

CONTENTS

Acknowledgements

Preface

PREFACE

Blow Your Little Tin Whistle is a biography of Richard
Clarke Sommerville, an educator, amateur actor, and artist, whose life and times spanned the last quarter of the
nineteenth century and six decades of the twentieth century. I first became aware of Richard Sommerville during
my first year of teaching at Lynchburg College. This book
is the culmination of my efforts to learn more about one
who has been called, the "Renaissance Man" and at times,
the "man of mystery," who felt at home in the arts, the
sciences, and the humanities, and who dedicated his life to
teaching and learning.

His story is not only of one man's personal struggle
for survival and his search for happiness, but also of
private education in America told from his experiences.
During his time, public education at the elementary and
secondary levels was just beginning in his native state of
Virginia and in West Virginia where he grew up. At a time
when post-secondary education was in the throes of change,
Richard Sommerville became a teacher and taught at every
level. He held very definite views about what an education
should do for the individual. His education within the
home environment, his experiences within the educational
settings of his day, and his ultimate acceptance of his own
lot in life helped him, in part, to formulate these views.
Many of his views are as timely today as they were then.

At the age of fifteen, Richard went to school at
Hampden-Sydney College for Men. There he thrived
socially and excelled academically. During his studies at
Hampden-Sydney, reforms were occurring in education
across the country. Debates concerning the curriculum

were underway with one side arguing for classical education and for recitation and drills in the ancient languages of Latin and Greek, and in mathematics. Proponents of the "doctrine of formal discipline" held that such drills were necessary as a means of exercising the mind. Instruction was topic-driven. On the other side, proponents like John Dewey were leading the fight for education to be more student-oriented. Richard was educated within the classical model with its highly articulated curriculum which was being challenged elsewhere. Although he concentrated in Latin, Greek and mathematics, his studies introduced him to history, science, and philosophy. While his studies in moral philosophy sparked his interest in psychology, a discipline in which one day he would receive his doctorate, the teachings within moral philosophy with its emphasis on duty, obligations to society, and high moral ground influenced him for life.

While a student at Hampden-Sydney, Sommerville was involved with the literary and debate societies where he won many gold medals for his work, especially for writing essays. Dr. Elza Tiner, assistant professor of English and director of the Writing Center at Lynchburg College, has annotated Sommerville works and discusses the nature of the assignments which he might have encountered during his studies. Three examples of Richard Sommerville's essays are included in Appendix A.

The years following graduation were fraught with uncertainty and difficult times for Richard Sommerville. At the age of twenty, he embarked on a teaching career, but he developed tuberculosis. Young Richard's family sent him out West to sleep on the desert floor, then the only known cure for the disease. As he was expected to die, he was sent with little money and was forced to forage and beg for food. Although he recovered and returned to teaching, during most of his early years, he seemed a restless young man unable to settle. His health contributed to his restlessness, but he was searching for something more.

Finding himself at a crossroad following the end of World War I, Richard decided to study for his doctorate in the new discipline of experimental psychology at Columbia University. His era was considered "golden" by some, owing to the large number of well known faculty there who provided excellent education for the students. Interested in interdisciplinary studies, he studied higher education at Teacher's College, and philosophy and psychology at Columbia University. He received his doctorate in 1925 and at the same time taught in several liberal arts colleges from Arkansas to Tennessee.

Not until he arrived on the Lynchburg College campus in 1928 did Sommerville put down roots. There at the age of fifty-two he was able to develop his last career as a respected college professor teaching in the areas of education, philosophy, and psychology. Despite the hardship of the Great Depression of the nineteen-thirties when he lost his program, he managed not only to survive, but also to solidify his own philosophy of life. Encouraging his students to do the same, "because its helps one to know where one stands on important issues," he is well remembered for encouraging his students to accept themselves and to seek happiness from within.

Known within the community as an amateur actor and artist, his interests in community theater and in the art league were part of his definition of a well-rounded life. As a professor of aesthetics, he was keenly interested in helping his students to develop an awareness of the fine arts. His personal involvement, which allowed him to serve as a model for his students, was his means of socialization.

Although he was not famous within his field, Sommerville was a respected citizen of the community and a popular teacher. While he clearly could have gone for fame, he chose not to. Perhaps his personality more than any other characteristic led to his popularity. Perhaps his wisdom in counseling and guiding the young men and women in his classes made him different. Perhaps his philosophy of life and the fact that he encouraged his students to form a philosophy for living that endeared him to his students. Perhaps his acceptance of all people regardless of their lot in life made people so comfortable in his presence. More likely, however, his message encouraged his students to take pride in who they were, to believe in themselves, and to accept whatever calling in life they chose. He did not believe any calling in life was menial while other occupations were grand. All activities, as far he was concerned, were part of God's plan. His central message to his students was *to blow their little tin whistles* rather than seeking to blare trumpets, his way of telling them to accept themselves and seek happiness from within.

Richard Sommerville's expressions, "blow your little tin whistle" or "beat your little tin drum," reflected the spirit and perhaps the mission of Lynchburg College. The college has always been an institution that expects the middling to above average student to do his or her best, to rise to his or her full potential. Not all of us can be great stars in our respective fields and each must start from his or her own level. Hence, Richard Sommerville's advice is a reminder to us to be humble, to recognize our strengths and weaknesses, and to work within our own framework, for that is the true road to excellence. Thus his teaching emphasized his philosophy, which is the heart of the mission of Lynchburg College, and what makes it a truly great little college in its own way. His biography is a message to all students from a very special teacher.

Peggy Pittas

1

"THE JEWEL ON THE SOUTH BRANCH"

A Keen Memory

One of Richard Sommerville's earliest memories was a trip in the summer of 1881 with his cousin, Sallie Sommerville. He was five years old. Leaving White Post, Virginia, they traveled by horse and buggy the ten or so miles to Winchester where they boarded the B & O train and arrived at Keyser, West Virginia. There they spent the night in the Keys Hotel and the next day they completed the remaining forty-four miles of their long two-day journey by private carriage to Moorefield, West Virginia. The train ride was the only way by public transportation into the valley at that time. A few years later, public transportation included a train ride as far as Romney and then a four- or five-hour stage coach ride into Moorefield. These rides, hot and dusty in summer, cold in winter, could be shared alike by passengers, packages, and crates of chickens.

Young Richard's first train ride was taking him to spend the summer months with his uncle, Alexander

Sommerville, who lived at "Oak Hall," a very large farm in Hardy County. Three years later, at the age of eight, young Richard moved with his mother to live in Moorefield, the county seat. They left their home, "Sommer Villa," located in White Post and took up residence in the "Old Court House" located at the corner of Winchester Avenue and Franklin Street (now known as Elm Street). The home was a very large structure located next to the jail. Because they thought their new home resembled a French chateau, they called it the "Old Chateau." That name did not stick, however; today it is once again known as the "Old Court House."

To say that Richard Sommerville had a long and keen memory is an understatement somewhat analogous to saying that the Grand Canyon is a hole somewhere in Colorado. Known throughout his life for his quick mental powers, he was able to remember nearly all that he read, all that he heard, and all that he experienced. His was an exacting memory which could recall details. He liked details. He admired precision in all things, and he prided himself in his ability to think, speak, and behave exactly. He believed that permanent memories began at about age five, the beginning of the age of awareness for humans. His studies in the disciplines of psychology and education of his day taught this theory; his own experience confirmed it.

Nowhere is there a better illustration of Sommerville's ability to recall details than in an article that he wrote for *The Moorefield (West Virginia) Examiner.* At the age of eighty-one, he recounted not only the clear details of his early life in Moorefield, but also the names of the people who lived on each farm and in each house within the town. Moreover, he remembered the exact geographical relationship of each place to the other, and of course, he knew the area's history. His account appeared in an invited column titled "The Old Timer" on October 10, 1956. Included with the seven-column, full-page article, was a map of the town as it stood circa 1884. Sketched from memory, it contained some ninety-three businesses and homes. Although he said that his primary purpose was to tell something of what life was like in the eighteen-eighties, he also managed to weave lessons of history, geography, and family heritage into his recollections.

His characterization of the town providing a "serene and satisfying life" was a sentiment echoed by the late Amy Bowen Eby, his niece, in her memories of life in turn of the century Moorefield. Even though she moved to Chicago, she did not forget her roots. Well into her nineties, she expressed the sentiment that "people living in isolated areas or communities are not necessarily deprived, and ... that these small towns served to help form that basis upon which... [the country's]... subsequent greatness, power, and prestige would come to rest."[1] Her account of the customs, dress, and attitudes of the people around her, combined with Richard's recollections of the town's history and customs, the economy, and the introduction of such modern conveniences as the telephone, the car, and electricity, depicted a certain pride in their heritage. They appreciated the simplicity and serenity of rural living; they never felt themselves deprived, although there was never much money in those years. In their advanced ages, they loved to recall and to instruct others in history. Then again, a passion to learn and teach was characteristic of the Sommerville clan.

The life that Richard described was reflective of a small town surrounded by large and fertile farm lands owned by a rather stable population, many of whose ancestry dated back to colonial days. His litany of names of the eighteen-eighties included the descendants of several families such as the Vanmeters and the Kuykendalls who were directly descended from Issac Vanmeter and William Kuykendall, two of the original settlers who moved "southwestwardly from New York and Pennsylvania."[2] By the seventeen fifties, the names of Inskeep, Harness, McNeil, Welton, and Cunningham were prominent in the history of Hardy County. Several, for example the Cunninghams,[3] had come directly from the counties around Londonderry, Ireland, in the last half of the eighteenth century seeking religious freedom, as had the Sommervilles.

Memories of the Family

The name Sommerville is French in origin and has been traced back by family genealogists to Sir Gualtier (Walter) de Sommerville, a Norman knight who crossed the English Channel with William the Conqueror in 1066.[4] Despite a gap of some five hundred years when thousands of Somervilles inhabited the British Isles and much of the rest of Europe, the family line is traced to John Sommerville of Grasha, near Londonderry in Northern Ireland. He, according to Charles William Sommerville, Richard's older brother and an ardent genealogist, was a Presbyterian farmer whose ancestors were from Scotland.[5]

John had five sons who eventually emigrated from Scotland to the American Colonies. They were Joseph, Thomas, William, Alexander, and George, from whom Richard Sommerville was directly descended. Joseph and William came first in 1773, among the thousands of Scotch-Irish Presbyterians from the nine counties of Ulster who immigrated between 1772-1774 seeking religious freedom and relief from the persecutions by the English.

Over the century, Richard's forefathers, and all the other settlers who located in the Virginia territory then called the "back country," carved out large farming manors despite fighting Indians, and doing battle with Lord Fairfax, and later his heirs, to obtain deeds to their property.[6] Moreover, since the location was surrounded by mountainous terrain, entry into the Valley was difficult. Over the years, they built their churches, mainly Presbyterian, Brethren and Methodist denominations, their court houses, and their hotels. For protection, they had their voluntary Militia, the "Hardy Blues" and the "Juvenile Hussars." The "Jewel on the South Branch," as it was called, weathered many challenges. Then came the Civil War.

Moorefield's location was geographically aligned with the North, but the sentiments of the clear majority of citizens favored the Confederacy. The citizens had a long identity as Virginians. When the war broke out and Virginia seceded from the Union, Hardy County was part of the Old Commonwealth. When Governor Letcher called the various counties to form a militia, a very large number of the citizens of Moorefield and Hardy County answered the call. Hardy County was split in its sentiments, and the northernmost part of the county (now Grant County) was inclined to go with the Union, and a detachment called the "Hardy Blues" was reorganized. In the southern part of the county, the "Hardy Greys" was formed early in 1861. Over the ensuing years, the "Hardy Greys" and other militia from the region found themselves in service variously under the commands of Robert E. Lee, "Stonewall" Jackson, and Turner Ashby, among many others. A few did join the Union forces, but from this region, they were a definite minority.

In October of 1861, when the people of West Virginia ratified a plan for their new state, only 150 votes were cast by Hardy County residents, and all of them were for the new statehood. This vote was far smaller than the 1,655 voters who went to the polls in 1860 as so many were away fighting.[7] By 1863, when the state of West Virginia was formed, many citizens of Hardy County and Moorefield had either died in service to the Confederacy or were already assigned to various Virginia detachments deeply entrenched in the bitter fighting.

Hardy County's fertile valley known for its grains and abundance of "fat cattle" was a prized possession for both sides. Its location on the borders between the North and the South made it a bitter battle ground. The town of Moorefield "changed hands" more than a dozen times and the buildings were variously occupied by troops for both sides. By the war's end in 1865, when the soldiers came home from both sides, the majority of whom had served the Confederacy, they returned to a war-torn town that had a new state name. For many, it was difficult to change mentalities, especially since the Confederate veterans were now disenfranchised and faced drastic penalties. By 1866, Hardy County was split into two counties with the formation of Grant County, and they shared one representative to the state house for several years.

Although Richard made no reference to the Civil War in his account, Moorefield's identity with the South would certainly have been important to the Sommerville family who had moved away from the North into Virginia where his father had volunteered his services to the Confederacy. William (1827-1876), Richard's father, was born in Bloomery Mills (now the part of West Virginia called Bloomery) on a bounty of land that was awarded to his father James for services rendered in the War of 1812. As a teenager, William worked as a postmaster in the local general store. Although he originally thought of being a Presbyterian minister, he studied medicine at the Winchester Medical College and at the Jefferson Medical College of the University of Pennsylvania.[8] After finishing medical training, William returned to Bloomery Mills, joined Dr. John Sigsworth Guyer, and they established a large medical practice.

Richard's mother, Maria Louisa Aby, was born in Middletown on May 5, 1834. She was the thirteenth of fourteen children born to Jonas and Barbara (Hulett) Aby. Her father, a French Huguenot, had moved from Pennsylvania into Virginia, served in the War of 1812, and was a shoemaker by trade.[9] Educated in Middletown, Maria moved to Bloomery Mills to be the tutor to the children of Col. Robert B. Sherrard. He was a wealthy man, and as was the custom of the day, private tutors were hired for his children. Maria was the sister-in-law of Dr. Guyer and Col. Sherrard was an Elder along with William Sommerville in the same church.[10] This inter-connectedness of the proper family and friendship brought William and Maria together; they were married on May 29, 1856.

Although the William Sommervilles were to have a relatively happy life, the times did not provide for an easy one. The Civil War began in 1861, and by 1863 the area, considered homeland to five generations of Sommervilles, was divided politically and socially by the newly created state of West Virginia. Perhaps foreseeing the inevitable, in October of 1862, William moved with his family back within the borders of Virginia. After a brief stay in Middletown, they eventually settled in White Post where he purchased a home, naming it "Sommer Villa."[11]

William not only practiced medicine to the civilian population but also volunteered his services to the Confederate army as did his brother, Dr. Henry Clay Sommerville, who volunteered from Missouri. Exactly where William signed on and where he served is not well documented; however, he is listed as having been assigned to duty on October 12, 1864 at the Chimborazo Hospital

#5 in Richmond, Virginia. He was reassigned in early 1865; the location is thought to have been Staunton, Virginia.[12]

William returned to "Sommer Villa" at war's end, rebuilt his home, and began practicing medicine. For the Sommervilles, in this post-war era, life operated on the barter system. The doctor gave medical treatment in return for food and services. Richard's older brother, James, had as a regular chore to saddle his horse, travel around the country-side and collect the food for the family larder. William died at the age of forty-nine, his life cut short by the rugged life of the country doctor. He left a widow with seven living children, and no wealth; Richard was less than a year old. Born on October 12, 1875, at the end of the era that historians call The Era of Reconstruction, he never witnessed events of the war as had his three older sisters. He grew up hearing eye-witness accounts of battles in Virginia. One of his earliest heros is said to have been Robert E. Lee, to whom he would show respect throughout his life. He once said that he admired him for his integrity and strong sense of commitment to duty.

In 1867 a committee formed, whose members included an aunt and cousins, for the purpose of making a monument to those who had died in service to the Confederacy from Moorefield. The ceremony was always held near Memorial Day (originally called Decoration Day) and often it occurred on Robert E. Lee's birthday. This event involved the whole town, and the children including young Richard participated. Amy Eby, Sommerville's niece, called this day the "annual disappointment." She assumed that the plans were set by the local chapter of the Daughters of the Confederacy. In any case, it was never held on Sunday and took weeks of preparation. Loads of mountain laurel and evergreens were gathered from the nearby mountains and were combined with flowers grown in the local gardens. A wreath was made for each of the soldiers interred in the Confederate Cemetery.

> At 2 p.m. on the great day, the procession was formed, each boy and girl carrying a wreath aslant across their shoulders, and a bouquet in their hands. The marshals, spirited young men on equally spirited horses, wearing rich red silken sashes, rode along side to protect the young marchers from harm. The weather was hot, the wreaths heavy, but nothing was too good nor too much trouble for the honored dead. Arriving at the cemetery, each child stood at the headstone of a soldier's grave. At a given signal, the wreaths were lifted from their shoulders and placed aslant the headstones. Bouquets were placed flat on the grave. The very sincerity and simplicity lent it dignity. Usually a male quartet sang "Tenting Tonight" or some other sad but sweet soldier's song. A wreath was tossed in turn by the young men until it landed exactly as planned on the high top of the monument. A rope of evergreen which had been attached to the wreath, was wound around the monument, and fastened at the base. No speeches were made at the cemetery....[13]

Mrs. Eby could never remember a single incident of misconduct during this prayerful event because "feeling ran too deep."[14] Over the years this "prayerful event" in Moorefield also served to unite rather than divide the town. By the turn of the century, the old "Tenting Tonight" song was replaced by "My Country 'Tis of Thee" as both the Union and Confederate veterans came together to talk about how it was.[15]

Slowly but steadily, the citizens of Moorefield and Hardy County rebuilt after the ravages of the Civil War. In those days the farms were large. The primary crops of corn, oats, and hay were grown for profit as well as to feed the large herds of cattle, sheep, and hogs which were the economic mainstay of the area. The cattle were purchased in the West, fed in West Virginia and then shipped for sale in Baltimore. Often they were sent to Europe. Cash was available when the crops or cattle were sold. Otherwise, the farmers were carried by the merchants and accounts were settled maybe two or three times per year. It was also a barter economy as the people's lives were intertwined, not only by kinships, but by a cooperative sharing of the jobs necessary for living in such a geographically isolated area.

Memories of the Eighteen-Eighties

The farming economy operated on the lien or credit system. Sommerville remembered well the depression of the eighteen-eighties which hit Moorefield rather hard. As the town had economic ties to Europe, when the depression started in England, it was felt immediately in Moorefield. In order to purchase cattle and seed, the farmers borrowed with promissory notes, and other family members and friends endorsed the notes. During the depression, the banks called on the borrowers to make good on their debts, and according to Sommerville, since everyone was an endorser for everyone else's notes, "the whole system tumbled like a deck of cards."[16] Many lost their farms and were forced to move away, hoping to rebuild elsewhere, but most were saved by relatives and friends who bought out the homes and allowed the original owners to stay on to work off their debts.

Moorefield resembled a town in the old West. There were no paved roads, and cattle-drives occurred through the town's main thoroughfare. Also, herds of sheep were sometimes led through the streets. The town pump provided relief for the weary traveler and thirsty animal alike. Sommerville remembered that the town had no telephone until the mid-eighties, when "a line was extended from Romney up a back road east of the Trough. Dixon Alexander made the survey. At first there was only one receiving instrument in town, placed in one of the stores." Out of curiosity, people would go to the store and talk to a friend in Romney. They marveled that the voice sounded so near and natural. This phone was used mostly for transmitting telegrams. A boy like young Richard could pick up fifty cents by getting on a horse and carrying messages to some farm several miles away.

Just as the people were self-sufficient in their livelihood, they organized and created their own forms of entertainment. The cultural life in Moorefield in the eighteen-eighties included the literary, musical, and drama clubs where Richard's sisters, Annie and Ada, were active members, as was his future brother-in-law, C.B. Welton. Young Richard's love of amateur theatre started early when he became a member of the children's theater group. His first attempt at acting was at the age of ten, when he and his sweetheart, aged eight, acted out Little Miss Muffet for the MWG Club.[18] His part was to manipulate the spider as she played Miss Muffet. During his pantomime of a boy fishing, she poured the water over him. Presumably, that was not part of the script.[19]

Aside from acting, he was taken on as protégé of William Alexander, an artist who had studied in Paris, and who was a painter of horses. He lived part of the year in the Moorefield area and the rest of the time in Kentucky. He could be recognized as he carried a long staff and went about in a slouch hat and clothes that were never pressed. Aside from his sisters and his mother, Will Alexander was Richard's first art teacher.

There were jousting tournaments at "Oak Grove" where the young men would become the "Knights of Ferncliff" and compete for the three brass rings in order to crown their favorite girl as "The Queen of Love and Beauty." There were softball games, community picnics, and ice skating in winter.

Richard's lifetime corresponded with the development of many modern conveniences that people today take for granted. Throughout his life, Richard was impressed with developing technology. Later he referred to such advances as positive proof that civilization was progressive, growing ever more intelligent. He remembered the first house that had electricity, the first designed for indoor plumbing, and the first that had a furnace. His memory also included the first automobile, and later, the Greyhound Bus. Yet he still appreciated a fine saddle horse or a fine rig. Nor did the advances in transportation ever interfere with his propensity to walk, to take, as they were called, "pedestrian tours" where he loved to commune with nature.

At the age of twelve, young "Rich" went to work for his brother-in-law, Dr. Bowen, who owned one of the local drug stores, in addition to his medical practice. According to the store ledger (now available in the archives of the Hardy County Public Library), by 1889 "Rich" worked for seven dollars a month plus board. In April of that year he received a raise to eight dollars per month plus board. Apparently he kept the job until he went off to Hampden-Sidney Academy in 1891. According to his own account, he was able to "study some" on his own in between his assigned duties at the drug store. This rite of passage into young adulthood put an end to Richard's favorite pastimes of playing doctor to his sister's doll and building model sailboats.

"The Scholarly Habit and Appetite..."

The widow Maria Sommerville originally moved to Moorefield where she started a private school with her daughters, Ada and Annie. Richard once described it as a "kind of cooperative with teachers who were not hired by the county."[20] Here Richard received his early education until the age of twelve, when he went to work at the drug store. This school operated in direct competition with the public elementary school within walking distance of his home. However, the town had no high school, as public education beyond the seventh grade was not available in Moorefield until after the turn of the century. For generations, education had been important to the Sommervilles. Teaching was their means of livihood; learning was their way of life.

Like their parents, Richard and each of his siblings were educated in private schools. Obviously the parents and his older sisters had no choice because public education was not available for their generations. Richard's great-great grandfather, the immigrant George, was a school teacher in colonial Winchester, and it is said that many of the earliest settlers were his students. He was described as being a "very stern man, not showing much affection for his children nor allowing them to eat with him and grandmother."[21]

Stern or not, George was among the Scotch-Irish Presbyterians credited in many quarters for fostering education within the American colonies. Dale Robinson, in discussing the role of the various denominations on education in Virginia, wrote:

...Of the former group, most conspicuous by far for their achievements were the Scotch-Irish Presbyterians. These hardy folk early recognized the need for an educated clergy and laity; thus, wherever their houses and churches sprang up in the Valley or in the Piedmont, their "log colleges" were sure to follow in short order.[22]

These "log colleges" could take many forms, but the term "classical school" meant the study of Greek and

Latin, the fine arts, as well as the prescribed curriculum of history, natural and moral philosophy, mathematics and so on. According to Robinson, the curriculum at these classical schools essentially established the format of studies in the four-year liberal arts schools. However, the influence of the Scots and Scotch-Irish was far more pervasive for higher education than Robinson implied. According to Rand Evans, after the founding of Harvard by the Puritans and up to the time of the American Revolution, of the nine colleges founded in the American colonies, six were under the control of the Presbyterians. By 1851, they controlled directly or indirectly two-thirds of the colleges. By the time of the Civil War, of the one hundred and eighty-two colleges in the United States, the Presbyterians directly or indirectly controlled forty-nine.[23]

The emphasis on classical education did not receive unanimous acclaim nor for that matter, were the log schools highly regarded. In 1935, Frederic Morton presented his views:

> Until 1870 all the educational training received by the young people of Winchester came through the private schools. So far as these were of academic grade, the instruction was too bookish and there was an undue emphasis on Latin and Greek. The teaching was in fact more ornamental than practical. Its avowed aim was to impart culture to the youth of both sexes rather than to fit them for specific lines of employment in a workaday world. But though deficient in the latter particular, the exacting drill did impart a good deal of mental discipline and mental grasp. And if the schools of lower grade seems (sic) like the Dark Ages to the pedagogue who tries to follow the niceties, such schools were nevertheless quite practical in their day and time. The teaching was not sugar coated. It was switched into the pupil whenever the teacher deemed the switching necessary, and the use of hickory oil was sustained by public opinion.[24]

Public education as it is known today was passed in

the Virginia legislature in 1871, four years before Richard was born. Then it was considered controversial and received opposition for many reasons and from many quarters. For example, many parents thought that education was a family responsibility, not the business of the state. Others were concerned lest public education lead to integration of the races.[25] Apparently, the establishment of free public education did not immediately affect the Sommervilles as they continued their strong family tradition of education within the home environment. During the years at White Post, the three eldest daughters graduated from Fairfax Hall. Originally known as the Winchester Female Academy and founded in 1800, this school was reorganized and renamed Fairfax Hall in 1869. The founders of these two large classical schools were Presbyterian ministers of Scotch-Irish descent.[26]

Following their formal education, the sisters held their own private school in the family home at "Sommer Villa." The three eldest sisters, Louisa, Ada, and Annie, taught the younger children. The pattern was for the children to study within the home environment until the age of fifteen or sixteen and then they attended a private academy. For the three Sommerville brothers, Charles, James, and Richard, this sequence provided a foundation for college and university educations. For the sisters, Louisa, Annie, Ada and Sophie, it was their path to becoming competent teachers. With the exception of James, who was a successful businessman and lawyer, all were teachers at some time in their lives; Charles and Richard were to become known as outstanding educators. The family emphasis on education and lifelong learning gave rise to one of Richard's favorite phrases; he admired those who showed "the scholarly habit and appetite."

The Sommerville family life was close knit with a mutual interest in painting, drawing, music, poetry, literature and acting. Their preference was clearly for the more "ornamental than practical" instruction, and they believed that a good education *should* aim to "impart culture to the youth of both sexes rather than to fit them for specific lines of employment in a workaday world."[27] This family interest in the arts led to lifelong avocations for the entire clan. When they were apart after marriage or when schooling separated this large family, they frequently wrote to each other with brief news and often included something about what they were reading. Paper was scarce, so they saved slips of paper; a used envelope was snipped and the reverse used to copy or pen poems they wanted to share, or it was used for sketching.

Richard remained close to his brothers and sisters as long as they lived and often lamented his fate of surviving all of them. After he left to study at Hampden-Sydney, he returned many summers to visit his mother and sisters, Annie and Louisa, as did his other siblings. Although Richard's mother moved from Moorefield to Front Royal, Virginia, during the early to mid-nineties, he continued to return to Moorefield to see his sisters. At these reunions, the family usually read a play, some poems, or a book. Dr. Felix Welton, his nephew, remembers one summer when "Uncle Rich" and "Uncle Will" took turns reading aloud *Innocents Abroad* by Mark Twain for the family enjoyment. They loved literature, particularly the American classics, and the poetry was usually light verse; a family favorite was light verse by Wallace Irwin.

These family visits also included posing for portraits as Richard and his sisters preferred to do family portraits in life, not solely from photographs. Richard's habit was to use both photographs and a formal sitting in painting portraits. These portraits are all in the possession of heirs of his brothers and sisters.

The family reunions were special times and usually occurred in mid to late summer. The noon meal was the big meal of the day, after which the family would gather on the front porch for a short visit. Then everyone would retire for their afternoon naps. Baths were taken and all dressed for the evening in their best clothes. This custom was a natural reprieve from the high temperatures and daily chores of the morning hours. The evening hours provided the occasion for sitting on the front porch or for visiting with the neighbors and friends. Recalling so much gaiety and constant chatter, the nieces and nephews often wondered what there was to talk and laugh about until nearly midnight. When the poetry, painting, and conversations were spent, Richard and Sophie entertained the family, she at the piano and he with his flute. For this family, the arts were an integral part of their lives as a source of entertainment. None of them thought of themselves as artists or musicians or ever tried to make a living from these talents. If anyone liked them, that was simply flattering. Instead, they thought of themselves as educated people, which in their day meant an understanding and appreciation of the arts for a well-rounded life. The generations before television and instant art had to create their own forms of entertainment.

The Sommerville legacy included a strong religious faith, a commitment to patriotic duty and civic responsibility, as well as an insistence on education. Whenever they wrote about themselves, they emphasized their heritage of which they were most proud. Remarkably every biographical account either outlines their academic accomplishments or includes a commentary that describes them as being well-educated and lifelong students. Such were the family themes, and moreover, these were the themes that would mark the life of Richard Clarke Sommerville and for which he would be most remembered.

Young Richard with his dark auburn hair with a

"Rich" Sommerville — early 1890's
(COURTESY OF MRS. FELIX WELTON)

slight wave, brown eyes and fair complexion, had a happy childhood with fond memories on the "Jewel on the South Branch." He was only eight when his mother moved there and although he left at the age of fifteen, he was to return again and again and was always a popular guest.

Amy Bowen Eby described her uncle:

> ...The visits which succeeded each other, year after year, were always about the same. Uncle Richard was of an even disposition, dignified, reserved, tho' in no sense unfriendly nor unsociable; he was gentle, quiet-mannered, calm, kind, placid, not easily disturbed. He treated my mother with great deference, respect and politeness. She was the oldest and he was the youngest of the family. After the noon meal (or after supper) they would sit on the vine-covered side-porch and talk, apparently happy in each other's company. Uncle Richard would smoke a good cigar, sitting on a certain bench which overlooked the yard, and beyond that, the garden, and to this day the fragrance of a good cigar, or the sight of that old bench on the porch at home, will bring to me a vivid mental picture of Uncle Richard... For at least half of the years of those visits there were no radios or T.V.'s. They did not need them. They were quite capable of furnishing their own amusement. It was scholarly conversation, broken now and again by delighted laughter. They definitely had a sense of humor, and plenty of sensitivity. They knew what to say and <u>what not to say</u>. They had taste and judgement. Uncle Richard possessed all of these attributes, in abundance. It was a lovely life, and Uncle Richard was a delightful guest.[28]

He is remembered by his nieces and nephews as always being polite, dignified, always reserved and of an even disposition. His dress was meticulous and matched his speaking style, deliberate, precise and pleasing, although he always had a slight lisp. While he clearly enjoyed his childhood in Moorefield, as well as his visits, for some unexplained reason, he would always refer to White Post, where it is said that Lord Fairfax himself had supervised the implanting of the posts to mark the entrance to his estate, "Green Court," as home.

Notes

1. Amy Bowen Eby, *Amelia of Another Day*, (unpublished 1984), 4.

2. Richard Clarke Sommerville, "The Old Timer" *The Moorefield (West Virginia) Examiner*, (October 10, 1956): 5. Welton Family Papers.

3. Richard K. McMaster, *The History of Hardy County - 1786-1986* (West Virginia: Walsworth Press, Inc., 1986), 1-50.

4. The family appears to have disagreed over whether the name should be spelled with one m̲ or two m̲'s. Richard and his brother, Charles, insisted that two m̲'s were proper, but even Richard used one m̲ on occasion. His nephew, James, dropped the second m̲ because he said most Sommerville's did this. Therefore, when various family members are cited or discussed, two different spellings of the name will appear.

5. Charles William Sommerville was an ardent genealogist. In 1899 he mapped out the family tree. The papers are the property of Dr. and Mrs. Felix Welton, Black Mountain, North Carolina, hereafter referred to as the Welton Family Papers.

6. The area referred to as the "back country of Virginia" included all of the land west of the Blue Ridge Mountains in Virginia and all of present day West Virginia. The Sommerville brothers and subsequent generations moved back and forth between White Post and Winchester, Virginia, and places in Hardy, Harrison, and Hampshire Counties in West Virginia when they were all part of the Old Commonwealth.

7. McMaster, 237. For a more detailed account of the divisiveness of the Civil War on the county, see Alvin E. Moore, *History of Hardy County of the Borderland* (West Virginia: McClain Printing Company, c1963), Chapters 4 and 5.

8. The Winchester Medical College was originally chartered as The Medical College of the Valley of Virginia in 1822, but went

out of business within five years. In 1846 it was rechartered, renamed, and relocated on a plot of land west of Stuart Street in Winchester where is survived until the Civil War when it was burned to the ground in the Battle of Winchester. (Frederic Morton, *The Story of Winchester in Virginia* [Virginia: Shenandoah Publishing House, 1935], 238-239).

9. *History of Virginia 5* (Chicago and New York: The American Historical Society, 1924), 71.

10. Robert B. Woodworth, *A History of the Presbytery of Winchester (Synod of Virginia 1719-1945)* (Virginia: The McClure Printing Company, 1947), 68, 148, 359-360.

11. Stuart E. Brown, Jr., *Annals of Clarke County Virginia Old Homes, Families, Etcetera* (Virginia: The Virginia Book Company, c1983), 218.

12. *Confederate Consolidated Index* (Washington, D.C.: The National Archives), MC 253 Roll 449 File 29.

13. Amy Bowen Eby, 55.

14. Feeling ran deep in her family. Her father, Dr. William Brounly Bowen, a VMI cadet, first fought with the Warren County Cavalry, commanded by his uncle, then with Turner Ashby's Cavalry. After matriculating at Virginia Military Institute in 1862, he was a cadet-private in the Battle of New Market, and then joined Mosby's Rangers where he served until the end of the war. (William Couper, *The V.M.I. New Market Cadets Biographical Sketches of all members of the Virginia Military Institute Corps of Cadets who fought in the Battle of New Market, May 15, 1864,* [Virginia: The Michie Company, 1933], 28).

15. Richard K. McMaster, 241.

16. Richard Sommerville, 5.

17. Ibid.

18. MWG is presumed to stand for Moorefield Wee Group.

19. Libbie Keeton and Reggie Thomas, "Dr. Richard Clarke Sommerville," *The Prism*, (May, 1946): 6-7.

20. Jackson Darst, "Behind That Desk - Richard Clarke Sommerville," *The Prism 7* (2 December, 1943): 9, 16.

21. James Sommerville, *Somerville Family of White Post, Virginia*, (unpublished: Welton Family Papers), 1-20.

22. Dale Robinson, *The Academies of Virginia (1776-1861),*

(Richmond: The Dietz Press, Inc. 1977), 28.

23. Rand B. Evans, "The Origins of American Academic Psychology," *Explorations in the History of Psychology in the United States*, in Josef Brožek, ed. (Lewisburg: Bucknell University Press 1984), 33.

24. Frederic Morton, *The Story of Winchester in Virginia*, (Virginia: Shenandoah Publishing House 1935), 238.

25. For a lengthy discussion on the deliberations surrounding the establishment of free public education from the conservative point of view, see R.L. Morton, *Virginia Since 1861* (Chicago: The American Historical Society, 1924), 221-225, 228.

26. Robert B. Woodworth, 343-344.

27. See note 24.

28. Letter to Dr. Mervyn Williamson from Amy Bowen Eby, 28 January 1972. Williamson Papers. Lynchburg College Archives.

2
The Hampden-Sydney Years

The School's Mission

At the age of fifteen, Richard enrolled in the preparatory program of Hampden-Sydney College. Sommerville's choice of Hampden-Sydney was true to his Presbyterian Heritage. Founded by the Presbyterians, many of whom were of Scotch-Irish descent, it was opened as a college on January 1, 1776 and has held sessions continuously to this day. Although a charter was requested, the Revolutionary War intervened so that the actual charter was delayed until 1783. The college founder, Samuel Stanhope Smith, patterned the curriculum after the model of Princeton University. Owned by the Hanover Presbytery, the school is now the second oldest in Virginia and the tenth oldest in the country. By Sommerville's time, it had become a symbol of the Presbyterian tradition in Virginia.

Richard's brother, Charles, had completed his A.M., A.B. and B. Sc. degrees at Hampden-Sydney and was also studying at Union Theological Seminary then located on the grounds at Hampden-Sydney. At the time of Richard's enrollment, he was a professor of Latin and German. Their brother-in-law, Cleland B. Welton, had been at least the second of his generation to study there; his father, Felix Branson Welton, had graduated from the theological school, and subsequent generations, including Felix Burwell Welton, would study at Hampden-Sydney College as well.

During the years that Richard was a student, Hampden-Sydney had already established a very clear mission:

> Hampden-Sidney (as the college name was then spelled) professes to be a college merely, and not a university. She retains a curriculum of study which long and varied experience has proved to be best adapted to effect a liberal education, as distinguished from education of a purely business or professional character.[1]

The students were further advised that they would be prepared to attend professional schools "of the highest grade" or be "fitted for the proper discharge of the duties of enlightened citizens." Hampden-Sydney's mission was very clear that its purpose was to first prepare the young men as citizens and if they so chose, they could seek further career training elsewhere. The school did not see its mission to train students in careers at an age too young for them to choose wisely.

Whatever the student's choice in life may have been, the curriculum was highly structured for the entire four years. The catalogues made it clear that while a more extended course of study may be valuable, the student was expected to achieve a thorough mastery of the specified texts and subject areas as defined by the faculty. The school summarized its position as follows: "As everything cannot be taught within four years to a youth of ordinary abilities, the attempt to do so is not made; but rather to do well and thoroughly what is professed to be done."[2]

By including the phrase..."a youth of ordinary abilities," Hampden-Sydney College did not see itself as an elitist school, but as a school where the average young man could improve himself and become a useful citizen. In retrospect, the school was not educating young men of ordinary abilities.[3] As post-secondary education was not necessary in those days, the students' backgrounds had to be rooted in a family setting where higher education was highly valued, failure was not tolerated, and studying was a serious business. The student of ordinary ability would not have seen value in the study of poetry and prosody in English, much less in the study of classical Latin and Greek. Moreover, Sommerville was a student during the severe depression years which had heavily affected the agricultural community, and many of his classmates came from families whose livelihood depended on farming. There simply was not much money to spend frivolously.

...As a Means for Training the Mind...

The college's stated mission and the course of studies described a school steeped in the old Scottish tradition of the "doctrine of formal discipline." This doctrine held that certain academic disciplines such as mathematics, Latin, Greek were worthwhile because they trained the many faculties of the mind. These separate faculties had to be exercised like muscles. According to this theory, the classics and mathematics were the best suited for exercising the mind; thus drills in these areas were essential. The purpose of this discipline was to prepare the mind, making it sharper, so that other unrelated materials could be learned more quickly. Within this model, education was topic-oriented as opposed to student-oriented. However, the "doctrine of formal disciplines" was being seriously questioned while Sommerville was a student within this tradition.

In those days, students without formal high school training were admitted as long as they showed academic promise. Richard was one of these. The admission requirements identified three areas in which the student should show proficiency: mathematics, Latin, and Greek. In addition to the basics of algebra and geometry, the applicant had to know declensions, conjugations, and the rules of syntax in both ancient languages. He was expected to be able to read from Caesar's *Gallic Wars*, Xenophon's *Anabasis,* or "any other easy classic."[4] All students had to appear for pre-testing on a specified day. If the professors felt that the student was not ready for the first year of studies, but was capable of completing the work later, then he would be assigned a tutor in mathematics, Latin and Greek. This tutor, always an alumnus of the college, was specially hired for the preparatory program.

The official transcripts for Sommerville's work in the preparatory program and for his four years of study have been lost, according to school officials. However, Sommerville listed his courses on his application for doctoral studies at Columbia University.[5] In the preparatory program he was enrolled in "a year's drill" in drawing, Greek, Latin, and algebra, and he was classified as a freshman for two years because of the "required drill." Within the four-year liberal arts program, all students had the same curriculum for the first two years with compulsory and some electives during the last two years of study. Because the curriculum and the degree requirements were so carefully laid out in the school's catalogues, knowing what Richard studied is not difficult.

During the first two years, primary emphasis was

placed on the three content areas of mathematics, Latin, and Greek. Each of these classes was held four or five times weekly. Mathematics included the study of algebra, geometry, trigonometry, and land surveying which was seen as an essential skill in those days. The catalogues indicated that "recitations" requiring original problems in mathematics were to be included. Latin studies included extensive drills in grammar, Latin prose composition, and the reading of original works, some of which were specified, such as Cicero's *Orations* and Virgil's *Aeneid* or Ovid's *Metamorphoses*. Greek studies included not only the study of grammar, and prose compositions, but Greek history, and geography as well. Original works from Xenophon's *Anabasis* and *Cyropaedia*, and Homer's *Odyssey* were included on the required reading list.

The curriculum also included the study of prosody, the study of rhyme schemes and metrical structure of poetry; during the second year, the course also included composition of Latin poetry. In English and literature courses, students used texts such as *Higher English Grammar* by Read and Kellogg; *Studies in English Literature* by Swinton; *Word Analysis* by Swinton; and *Primer of American Literature* by Richardson. They also studied Practical Rhetoric. In addition, all students were required to purchase a copy of *The Orthoëpist (School Edition)* by Alfred Ayres which was a text showing the correct pronunciation of words in the English language.

Biblical studies covered the history of the Old and New Testaments. For the first two years, the students studied the Old Testament (one hour each week), but the study of the New Testament was delayed until the junior year. Additionally, all students had to attend compulsory chapel and go to church on Sunday, as designated by the parents. If the parents failed to identify a church, then the faculty selected the appropriate church for the youngsters.[6]

Over Sommerville's four years of study, the grading system was consistent. Examinations were held twice a year at mid-term and at the end; however, monthly progress reports were sent home to the parents, not only telling them of the student's class performance, but also noting the number of absences from class. Final examinations were more important in determining grades which were defined on four levels. First Grade meant that the student had passed the course with distinction and that his name would be called out at the annual commencement exercises. The distinction of Second Grade meant that the student had passed the course and could proceed to the next level with his classmates. Third Class meant that the student had to sit for re-examinations and could pass the course only if he then received a second class or higher grade. Fourth Class meant that the student had failed the class and was not eligible for re-examination.[7]

During the junior and senior years compulsory studies were prescribed for all students regardless of their individual programs.[8] However, students also took electives which were chosen from the same content areas specified in the compulsory studies. These elective courses actually determined the type of degree awarded. The college awarded four degrees: 1) the Bachelor of Arts (A.B.); 2) Bachelor of Science (B. Sc.); 3) Bachelor of Literature (B. Lit.); and 4) the Masters of Arts (A.M.).

Mastery of the first two years of study was essential for matriculating into the upper level courses. All degrees could be completed in the allotted four years except for the master's degree which meant a fifth year of study. Richard Sommerville graduated in 1896, after five years of study including the "year's drill," with both the A.B. and A.M. degrees, with First Class Honors, and as the Valedictorian of his graduating class. The master's degree meant that he had successfully completed all required and all elective courses in moral philosophy, physical sciences, mathematics, Latin, Greek, English, political science, history, French, and German.

Sommerville first encountered psychology in the moral philosophy courses. This was still rather commonplace in some liberal arts schools even though psychology as a separate course and as a formal discipline was being instituted elsewhere on American college campuses. Psychology was seen as a part of moral philosophy in 1894 just as it had been defined by the college founder, Samuel Stanhope Smith, more than a hundred years previously. According to Rand Evans, Smith introduced psychology into the curriculum in nineteenth-century American colleges.[9] He believed that the study of the faculties of the mind should include the study of logic and moral philosophy. Smith saw moral philosophy as:

> ...an investigation of the constitution and laws of mind, especially as it is endowed with the power of voluntary action, and is susceptible to the sentiments of duty and obligation....The science of moral philosophy begins with the study of the human mind—its sensations, perceptions, and generally, its means of acquiring knowledge—its sentiments, dispositions and affections, and generally, its principles of action or enjoyment—its present state, and reactions to other beings—its future hopes and fears.[10]

According to Evans, Smith's method of science was inductive, and he had no difficulty accepting the more empirical teachings of John Locke. Apparently so did the Rev. Richard McIlwaine, D.D., president of Hampden-Sydney and the professor of moral studies and Bible studies; he also taught psychology as a first course in moral science, followed by writings by John Locke. Logic was taught as a separate topic and was optional to some of the undergraduate students, but not to the graduate students.

During the senior year, in addition to Porter's *Elements of Moral Science*, the curriculum included additional study in the history of philosophy and the history of civilization.[11] All of this was to have influence on Sommerville. Although he eventually received his doctoral degree in psychology with a different emphasis, and took additional courses in philosophy, years later he set a program that resembled the thinking of Samuel Stanhope Smith and Richard McIlwaine. This program placed emphasis on the study of the human mind "especially as it is endowed with the power of voluntary action, and is susceptible to the sentiments of duty and obligation...." Throughout his life, Sommerville believed that the purpose of education was to train useful citizens who, having first developed personal competencies, then concerned themselves with personal duty and social obligations. Obviously, he learned early.

As an undergraduate, Sommerville concentrated in Latin, Greek, and mathematics, and the college catalogues indicate that a majority of the students enrolled at Hampden-Sydney in those years also completed this program. His studies in mathematics included course work in differential calculus, integral calculus, advanced study of analytical and solid geometry, as well as the study of the history and philosophy of mathematics. The advanced Latin studies included not only drill in grammatical structures of poetry and prose, but also the study of the original works of such writers as Tacitus, Terence, and Plautus. The student was told quite clearly that the final exam in the senior year would include an 'extempore Latin composition'.[12] His curriculum in Greek not only included the study of grammar and prose composition, but also placed a heavy emphasis on the study of Homer and his writings, Plato's *Apology*, and the works of Sophocles and Heredotus, among others. Although Richard later taught Latin in elementary school, his studies in classical Greek and Latin provided him a lifetime of reading material as he was known to have read poetry in these two languages for pleasure throughout his adult life.

By the time Sommerville enrolled, Hampden-Sydney allowed the study of modern languages. Any student working toward the Bachelor of Arts degree could substitute the study of French and German through the second years for <u>one</u> of the ancient languages in the third and fourth years. All other degrees required that the student complete all course work including the specified translations in these two languages. Thus, in addition to all of the required work in Latin and Greek, Sommerville completed two years of German and two years of French. Later in his life, he became professor of French at Arkansas College even though his only formal credentials were his two years of study at Hampden-Sydney. However, Richard had grown up with exposure to the French language as his mother and his sisters all spoke the language.

Aside from the studies as described above, Sommerville's two degrees meant that he also completed courses in chemistry, astronomy, physiology, geology, kinematics and dynamics, and physics. He took advanced seminars in atomic theory (obviously a theoretical seminar) and chemical calculations. History included the study of England, the United States, American politics and government, as well as the South. Political science also included political economy. Additionally, all students had to read Woodrow Wilson's *The State*. Studies in English covered Elizabethan Literature, Eighteenth Century Literature, Old English grammar, (so that the student could read *Beowulf*) and the works of Shakespeare and Chaucer, among others.

Richard was a happy and involved student at Hampden-Sydney and thrived in the academic as well as the social life of the campus. The existing records of the college archives reveal a zealous young man who threw himself into the social and academic organizations. Although he had gone to school thinking about studying for medicine, he belonged in academia. Whether the decision was a conscious one or not, he trained to become an educator. Moreover, his formative years at Hampden-Sydney instilled in him the classical liberal arts traditions, which not only included a model of education, but also included a way of life, of thinking, and of socializing. The nineteenth-century model of higher education then emphasized personal excellence, the training of gentlemen scholars, loyalty and duty, and a healthy respect, if not near reverence, for society's recognized masters of the arts and the sciences. The apprentice Sommerville could easily be recognized as the Sommerville of the twentieth century, the master of all of these qualities.

....As a Means of Socialization...

Aside from the formal classes, student social life encouraged membership in the literary societies. These literary societies actually served as fora where the men of Hampden-Sydney could demonstrate their academic acumen. The two societies, the Union and the Philanthropic, were run by the students. Membership was decided by formal vote of the group. Although designed for forensics and literary pursuits, they provided a means for personal improvement in reading, in writing, and in debating skills. "After joining one society or the other, it is advisable for the students to work earnestly and endeavor to excel, exciting generous rivalry among their fellows and gaining much good to all parties concerned." Such was the counsel to the incoming students in 1894.[13]

The constitution, laws, officers, and all particulars were held *sub rosa*, a policy Hampden-Sydney men held firmly. This meant that all meetings were closed to nonmembers and no proceedings were discussed on the outside. Membership also meant that students could live and study in the society halls and have use of the societies' libraries which were originally separated from the college library. The students bought the library books with the money received from fines, dues, and taxes. From the same funds they paid for the insurance to cover the value of the building and its furnishings. By personal labor, Sommerville's predecessors built and furnished the societies' halls.[14] Thus, a sense of ownership was felt by all even in his generation. By the time that Sommerville arrived, all three libraries had merged and the school boasted that over ten thousand volumes were available to the students who numbered one hundred and forty-seven in his freshman class.

Pledges to the chosen literary society created an immediate identity which not only meant personal prestige but also obligations of moral conduct and sincere participation. All members had to debate, make speeches (declaim), write essays, short stories, or poetry, and perhaps read a selection for others to enjoy. While there was a minimum requirement for each activity, the pledge could do more. Should a student refuse to participate, he was summarily voted out of the group by formal action.

Elected officers present at meetings included the following: the president or presiding officer; the censor who kept the rolls and brought those for improper conduct before the group for sanctions by formal proclamation; two clerks who kept the minutes and the speaking schedule; the treasurer who kept tally of dues and fines; the corrector whose task, it is presumed, was to check the submissions for proper grammar, punctuation, and spelling; the reader who evaluated the work; and the marshall whose duties were never made clear in the minutes. From time to time other officers appeared in the minutes, but they were never defined.

Above all else, the student wanted to be the annual gold medalist in either debate, literary writings, or in public speaking. Such is recorded many times, but expressed well by Captain A.M. Fauntleroy, M.D., a naval surgeon:

> ...The greatest honors in my day were the medals given by the Literary Society each year. I strove earnestly for the Freshman Declaimer's and the Sophomore Debater's Medal, but I was far outclassed by Lee Trinkle....In this connection I spent all and by, many hours in the near-by woods trying to improve my delivery and incidently shivering the adjacent timber with my histrionic outbursts....[15]

Both Richard and his brother, Charles, were active members of the Philanthropic Society. During his Freshman year, on January 8, 1892, Richard sought membership "by his own head"; his request was granted. He threw himself vigorously into the group as evidenced by *The Minutes of the Philanthropic Society*. On January 22, just fourteen days after induction, he gave a declamation, a six-minute speech on some prepared topic without notes. On that day, he also participated in his first formal debate. The topic was: "Resolved that an infidel should not hold public office in the U.S." Siding with the affirmative, his team won the debate by vote of the membership and by decision of the referee.[16]

On January 29, he gave his second declamation (topics were seldom recorded except when the clerk decided it was noteworthy). February 2 found him debating for the negative: "Resolved that railroads and telegraph lines should be in the hands of the government." This was a hotly fought contest, but the negative side prevailed by a vote of eighteen to eleven.[17] Voluntary declamations continued at every meeting on February 26, March 18 and 25, and April 8. In addition, he was appointed to "decide the merits of the debate" at the February meeting. On March 25, he debated for the affirmative: "Resolved that monopolies and trusts should be crushed." This time, however, the negative side won by vote of twenty-six to eleven.[18]

During his second year, Sommerville continued the same active pace. He gave voluntary declamations regularly at the bi-weekly meetings. Sometimes he read a composition or selections for the edification of the group. In addition, he participated in debates on some topics with results as follows:

1. "Resolved that indications point to a Democratic success." Arguing for the negative, his side won 36 - 10.
2. "Resolved that the Indian has as much right to vote as the Negro." Arguing for the affirmative, Sommerville squared off against Lee Trinkle, the future Governor of Virginia. No decision was recorded.
3. "Resolved that the results of the efforts to reach the North Pole are incommensurate with the loss of life and money." Arguing for the affirmative, his side won by a vote of 21 to 8.
4. "Resolved that Hawaii should not be admitted to the Union." Sommerville argued for the negative which lost by a vote of 31-5.[19]

In the fall of each year the group reviewed and decided who had won the gold medal for the previous year. Sommerville was nominated on September 23, 1892, but lost on the first ballot. Sometimes, two or three ballots were cast before a winner was declared. The same procedure was followed for the election of officers. Balloting simply continued until a winner was declared by majority vote.

Sommerville won the Debater's Gold Medal for his sophomore year. Also during that year, he was nominated for several offices, but lost all of the elections. However, during his junior year, he was elected as clerk and kept the minutes for the entire year which was unusual as the officers were changed regularly throughout the school term. During that same year, he won the Essayist Gold Medal. On April 6, 1894 he was elected president and served in that capacity until October 12, 1894. While serving as president, he continued to read favorite selections, to debate, and to give speeches. The *Minutes* of October 19, 1894, record that "Mr. Sommerville spoke a spirited oration on the impropriety of erecting a monument to John Brown."[20] Finally, on November 9, 1894, and in his senior year, he won the Senior Orator's Medal on the second ballot by a vote of 27-18.

By November 9, 1894, he apparently had finished the allotted time as a full member and along with ten others was moved to honorary membership. While his position as an honorary member precluded him from weekly and bi-weekly participation, he was elected as one of the three Hampden-Sydney representatives to the State Collegiate Oratorical Contest held in June of 1895 in Richmond, Virginia.

While remaining at the top of his class and attending bi-weekly and sometimes weekly meetings of the Philanthropic Society, he should have had little time for other activities, but such was not the case. He maintained an active membership in the Greek letter society, *Beta Theta Pi*, a social fraternity whose purpose was to improve literary exercise and cultivate social life. He was Hampden-Sydney's representative at the national convention held in Chicago on July 23-27, 1895.[21]

During his sophomore year, he was a member of *Theta Nu Epsilon*, another fraternity whose real purpose was not publicized. A note in the *Hand-Book* said that it drew principally from the fraternities and selected "those of congenial dispositions who are ambitious in class affairs." Membership was open only to sophomores, and names were held secret.[22]

Sommerville worked as an assistant college librarian in both his junior and senior years. He was also a member of the college Historical Society in his senior year. The stated purpose of this society was to study the history and literature of Virginia. Additionally, he was a member of the Press Club, a group who represented hometown newspapers and the representatives were responsible for sending newsworthy information from Hampden-Sydney to those papers. Ironically, Sommerville represented the Lynchburg, Virginia, newspapers, *The News* and *The Daily Advance*, which would one day feature him rather than print his news releases.

Young student Sommerville had a lighter side. A review of the *Kaleidoscope*, the college annual, shows that he was involved in many organizations designed for relaxation and recreation. He was the general manager (1893) and played the banjo for two years in the Hampden-Sydney Banjo and Guitar Club along with C.A. Sydnor who was to become his lifelong friend. Both played in the Capt. Tin-pan Brigade, which gave an annual event called the callithump (Greek "Kallos" meaning beauty, plus "thump" referring to sound). This event was a serenade of horns, tin pans, a bull-fiddle, and anything else which made a loud noise. The students would steal quietly through the night and arrive at professor's home to serenade them.[23] The 1894 *Kaleidoscope* also lists the United Order of Red-Heads to which Sommerville belonged. Apparently six members of his class had red hair, so they formed an order. Among the members were Star Mason, R.W. Dupuy, J. Gray McAllister, and C.H. Licklider. Of these red-heads, J. Gray McAllister became the sixteenth president of Hampden-Sydney (1905-08).

In 1885, Richard's brother, Charles Sommerville, had been one of the founding members of the student chapter of the Y.M.C.A. In Richard's era, he had become the faculty advisor who chaperoned all social and religious events. The primary purpose of the chapter was to conduct evangelical and mid-week prayer services as well as organize lectures, which were regularly held. Both men's earliest experiences with this organization during these years served as a prelude to their later service during World War I. As a student, Richard held office, serving as the treasurer in his junior year and as vice-president in his senior year. Also during his senior year, he was the associate editor of the *Student's Hand-Book*, a forerunner of today's student handbook, *The Key*.

As indicated earlier, literary and Greek societies were the focal points of student life. Just as in today's colleges and universities, all extra-curricular activities were controlled by the students. They alone were responsible for the physical upkeep of their fraternities and societies. However, important differences included no central governing body as each group and each student were responsible for self-policing. As well, no drinking was allowed and the penalty for this violation of the moral code was permanent expulsion. The near-by town of Farmville was off limits to students except for special occasions when the town formally invited them. Trips to the Farmville Normal School for Women (now Longwood College) were likewise not allowed except on special occasions.

The senior students assumed responsibility for advising the new students and the *Student's Hand-Book* included candid advice on etiquette.

1. Don't be fresh—just keep quiet, for a while, at least.
2. Don't tell an old student what he ought to do, or how to do it.
3. Don't use a nickname until you are given that liberty.
4. Don't express an opinion before it is called for.
5. Don't be familiar—a little dignity is greatly admired.
6. Don't be frightened at everything, nothing will hurt you.
7. Don't be childish—play the man.
8. Don't be profane, unless you desire the utter disgust of the very large majority of students.
9. Don't ask too many extraneous questions or you will regret your verbosity.
10. Don't break all the rules and wonder why it is you are so unpopular.
    Exercise your common sense and you will be respected by all.[24]

In Sommerville's time, the students lived in a residence, then called College Building, now known as Cushing Hall, or they boarded in private homes on or near the campus. During his first year, Sommerville lived in the home of Dr. Blair who was the professor of Latin language and literature and German. The home has long since burned, but the site is still marked today by a walkway which begins across from the science building and simply ends two buildings down from the library. The unsuspecting pedestrian might indeed pause and try to envision where the walkway once led.

The rooms in College Building where Sommerville lived during the last three years (he boarded with his brother during his second year) were either furnished by the students themselves, or arrangements could be made with the school. They typically contained two or three straight back chairs, a table, two beds, and a washstand with a bowl and pitcher. On the corner shelf could be found a pail which was filled every morning with water by a servant. The rooms were heated by fireplaces and there was no indoor plumbing. Servants cleaned the rooms daily.

During Sommerville's time, the students were responsible for heating their own rooms. They could buy pine for $1.50 per cord or oak for $2.00 per cord. If they were economical, they could manage the winter at something just over five cords per winter. If they did not want either, then they could pay a servant to cut the wood for $.50 per cord. However, if they did not want wood, then there was coal. Stoves could be purchased from $3.00 up and the coal was $5.00 per ton.[25]

The students were also responsible for supplying their own lighting. They were instructed to buy a very good lamp which had a proper burner so that it would give off good light. The student was informed to keep a can of good quality kerosene in his room. And so, students of the Sommerville era went off to college with an axe and a kerosene lamp with good supply of kerosene. While they did not have to clean their rooms, they did have to supply light, heating, and furniture![26]

Enjoyed by all students during the Sommerville years, athletics were more like today's intramural sports programs. Football, baseball, and track were the three main activities. In 1895, the board of trustees gave approval for the teams to travel. This change was announced in the *Student's Hand-Book* along with the expressed hope that in the future, athletics would reach the same public position as the oratory and literary works for which the college was well known. The campus publications do not indicate that Sommerville participated in any of the team sports. Although he was fond of tennis and horseback riding, he liked to walk.[27]

Richard Sommerville always held his student days at Hampden-Sydney in high regard. He excelled academically, was tirelessly involved in the social life, and made friends for life. Much of what Sommerville experienced at Hampden-Sydney, including membership in the literary society with its emphasis on self-monitoring, a willingness to take a personal stand on issues and state it publicly, and learning to think for oneself, was to become part of his personal code of ethics. As will be seen later, he never lost an opportunity to guide subsequent generations in these matters. He believed one should form opinions after reflecting on all the issues, stand up for personal beliefs, and above all else, do one's duty whenever called.

The Student Writer
Co-authored by Elza C. Tiner

While Sommerville was a student at Hampden-Sydney, the number of medals given for forensics, creative writing, and public speaking indicate that literary skills were highly prized. Although most of the evidence for his activity in these areas is in college documents and lists of names, Sommerville's own voice comes across in his student writings. Three essays, published in *The Hampden-Sidney Magazine*, and preserved in the Hampden-Sydney Archives, are reprinted in Appendix A.

The literary magazine offered students plenty of opportunities to learn the publication process. From April through December 1894, Sommerville was editor of "Alumni Notes", a section which provided information about Hampden-Sydney graduates. In the following term, he was put in charge of "Exchanges," reviews of student publications from other colleges. Yet, Sommerville must have preferred creative writing to his duties as editor. In the last issue of his senior year, May-June 1895, feeling nostalgic after graduation ceremonies, he reveals his preferences for private, creative thought. Nevertheless, while he writes tongue-in-cheek, his reverence for duty is evident:

> On the day after Commencement one feels more like talking of sighs and tears and faded roses than writing dry Exchange comments. Indeed if it were left us to choose, we should turn from our table in disgust, and wandering up and down the deserted corridors, would indulge in dismal meditations on the vanities of life and the sorrows of mortal men. However, it must be so; for the editor-in-chief is glaring at us across his desk and giving vent to sundry uncomplimentary remarks about people who neglect their duties and put others to great trouble in consequence, while the business manager has just left the office threatening to turn things upside down if the manuscripts are not sent to press immediately. So we heave a sigh for the things that were or might have been, and wearily turning to the piles of exchanges, begin the disagreeable task.[28]

During his senior year, Sommerville was elected editor in chief but served only one month, just long enough to welcome students back from summer holidays. Although he probably spent most of his time with upperclassmen, he maintained a genuine concern for the younger students. His editorial offers comforting advice: "Don't be afraid of a little homesickness." Such a feeling is an indication of a "good and noble nature" because it is caused by "regret of the absence of friends." No one can be considered noble if he forgets his friends as soon as they are gone.[29]

By the time the November edition was published, Sommerville had resigned his post as editor in chief. H. I. Brock took his place. The editorial ran only the statement that Sommerville had resigned against the will of the members "notwithstanding the most strenuous effort to prevent such a misfortune."[30] No reason was given for his resignation. However, Sommerville continued to publish his essays in the literary magazine.

The essays reflect his personal ethics, faith, and love of nature. Insistence on responsibility or duty was one of Sommerville's primary values. His ideals were based on his faith in the potential of humanity, an attitude he maintained throughout his lifetime. In spite of his youthful idealism, his essays were always derived from real sources: his readings, observations, and understanding of human nature. He must also have identified with the Virginia landscape, and particularly the mountains, as they are so often mentioned in his writings.

An article in *The News* of Lynchburg reported on Wednesday, August 29, 1894 that "Professor Summerville (sic) of Hampden-Sydney and his brother passed here this A.M. on a pedestrian tour. They had walked 100 miles and were in good plight and spirit. After viewing the sunrise (the Peaks, Bedford County, Va.) went on their way to Natural Bridge."[31] The two men were actually walking home to Clarke County at the time, as they were between sessions.

On this journey, Richard and his brother Charles probably passed the stone memorial for a slave who drowned while trying to rescue passengers in a canal boat on the James River. The stone marker read: "In memory of FRANK PADGET a coloured slave, who, during a freshet in James' River, in January 1854, ventured and lost his life, by drowning, in the noble effort to save some of his fellow Creature's, who, were in the midst of the flood, from death."[32]

In 1953, the *Virginia Cavalcade* published Robert L. Scribner's photographs of the monument and his account of Frank Padget's heroic deeds. Scribner's article was based on a story which appeared in the *Lexington Gazette*, January 26, 1854, five days after Padget's death. The monument is (or was, as residents of the area claim that it is not visible now) located next to the railroad tracks on the north bank of the James River in Balcony Gorge, northwest of Glasgow.

In January 1854, when the rivers were high from heavy rains, one Captain Wood tried to take his boat, the *Clinton*, across the mouth of the North River (now the Maury). The towline broke, and the boat was swept into the James River. Four crew members made it to shore, and three went over the Mountain Dam and drowned. The captain and several members of his crew jumped onto the White Rock in the James River; the rest remained in the boat as it headed downriver and finally got caught on a rock near the Tobacco Hills. As the boat cut loose again, one man jumped onto another rock, where he remained by himself. A group on the shore, led by Frank Padget, found another boat and collected those stranded on the White Rock and in the boat farther downstream. When they set out to assist the lone man on the rock, the rescue boat crashed and capsized. Five crew members made it to shore, but Frank Padget, the man he set out to rescue, and one other, named Bob, drowned. According to Scribner, Captain Edward Echols, one of those rescued by Padget, sent the story to the Lexington paper and had the stone monument erected.

Whether or not Richard knew the story behind the inscription on the monument, it moved him to write an essay on the theme of courage. When he returned to college in the following fall, he developed an essay on heroism, for which he won the 1894 Gold Medal.[33] The theme of the essay may have been set by one of his English professors. The prompt probably requested that the students develop a theme on the topic of a "Golden Deed," an illustration of heroism or courage.[34] Sommerville may have recalled from memory the words on the monument, but he changed the name of the slave. His revision of the inscription reads:

IN MEMORY OF
JAMES PADETT

A colored slave, who lost his life by drowning, in the noble
effort to rescue from death some of his fellow-men, during a
freshet on James River.

The name "James" connects the river with the hero
who drowned in it. Although Richard probably had seen
the monument during the day, he creates a romantic scene
in moonlight: "One bright ray, pure and clear, fell on the
grave at my feet...."[35] As he imagines what happened
during the storm, he includes plenty of stage-effects: "The
black and awful night, the lurid glare of the lightning, the
ominous mutterings of thunder, the incessant downpour
of rain, the howling of the wind, the despairing cries of
drowning men, and above and through all, the sullen roar
of the river, rushing onward, sweeping all in its terrible
course."[36]

Titling his essay, "The Slave-Hero" and developing it from the "heroic deed" which belied the "short,
simple, modest inscription," he wonders about other ordinary heroes whose deeds have been forgotten: "How many
graves there are like this one, hidden away in the obscure
corners of the earth! How many great and heroic deeds lie
beneath the shifting sands of the desert, the rocks of the
mountains, the waves of the restless sea!"[37] From his
dramatic style, one can understand how Sommerville might
have been drawn to the theater during his later years in
Lynchburg.

The essay reveals Sommerville's lifelong values.
Three basic themes formed early in his life. The first is to
do one's duty. No matter what station one holds in life,
responsibility is a sign of nobility. If one dies while attempting a noble deed, then that person is a true hero.
Paraphrasing Charlotte Yonge's *Book of Golden Deeds*

and quoting Alexander Pope's *Essay on Man*, Sommerville writes:

> The true metal of a Golden Deed is self-devotion. It is the spirit that gives itself for others—the temper that, for the sake of religion, of country, of duty, of kindred, nay of pity even to a stranger, will dare all things, risk all things, endure all things, meet death in one moment; or wear life away in slow, preserving tendance and suffering.
>
> What, then, constitutes a great man?
> Pope has given us the answer:
>
> 'Who noble ends by noble means obtains
> * * * * that man is great indeed.'[38]

The second of his lifelong values concerns heroes as role models for the young. Using a syllogism to express his reasoning, he once wrote that young people need heroes because they most effectively represent ideals for action. Ideals are necessary for progress. Therefore, by definition, heroes are necessary for progress. In this regard, he disliked the tendency of twentieth-century biographers who so magnified "the brute crudities of life and the frailties of eminent men that they tend to rob human nature of its significance and dignity....For when ideals are shattered and heros toppled to the mire, what is left in life worth striving for except animal satisfaction?"[39]

The third theme is illustrated by his careful attention to the natural elements in his essay—the rushing water, the thunderous skies, and the description of wildlife. He also makes numerous references to mountains, ever present in the southwestern Virginia landscape. He often refers to the mountains as touched or kissed by the clouds. In "A Slave Hero" the weary traveller stops to look out toward the horizon, a place "where the clouds and mountains meet" and recalls the heroic stories his mother told him as a child. Through the images of nature, he connects the traveller's childhood memories with dreams for his own future. Thus he teaches his fellow students: just as the mountains are touched by the clouds, so can the ordinary man aspire to lofty ideals. As is seen in subsequent chapters, wherever he went and for whatever reason, he would notice first the natural wonders of the world.

Richard Sommerville's love of nature also shows in his retelling of an Indian legend. A semester before "A Slave Hero" appeared, he published "Oola-Ita." Like James Padett, the heroine of this story also sacrifices her life for a heroic ideal: loyalty to her lover. Quite possibly, in one of the English classes at Hampden-Sydney, students had been assigned to retell a legend in their own words, a writing exercise that has been handed down for generations. In this kind of assignment, the instructor would supply students with a short plot summary of a popular story. The student would be expected to retell the story in a new way, so that it would be fresh and pleasing to the readers. Minor alterations in plot, setting, and characters would be permitted, as would descriptive details, dialogue and commentary on the story. "Oola-Ita" is probably based on the legend, "The Maiden's Rock; or Wenona's Leap," a version of which was published in 1849 by Mary Eastman.[41]

As in Eastman's version, Sommerville opens with a geographical description of Lake Pepin, though with additional details which suggest that he might have seen the lake at some point, perhaps from a railroad car. While Eastman describes the dimensions of the lake as about twenty miles long and one to two miles broad, Sommerville further aids the traveller who does not know the area. He locates the lake about forty miles south of St. Paul. Eastman makes no mention of the railroad (probably not there in her time), the crescent shape of the lake, or the exact location of the rock from which the Sioux maiden leaped to her death.[43]

In Eastman's version, the heroine, Wenona, is wooed by Chaske, a Dakota brave renowned for his superior hunting and fighting abilities. Her parents approve of him, accept his gifts, and promise him their daughter. However, Wenona prefers another man of the tribe. On a hunting expedition, while Wenona's tribe is setting up camp below a cliff, her mother sees her standing at the edge of the rock, where she is singing. Before they can stop her, she protests that she would sooner die than marry a man she does not love and leaps off the cliff.

Sommerville alters "Chaske" to "Chiska" and makes this the name of the heroine's lover. The man to whom she is promised is an unnamed "old chief," while Chiska is described as one of the youngest members of her father's circle. The age contrast of the lovers, also not mentioned by Eastman, adds to the pathos of the story. "Oola-Ita", not mentioned in the list of common Dakota names in the introduction to Eastman's edition, is probably Sommerville's invention.

In the original, Wenona's mother discovers her daughter standing on the rock, and a group of hunters, including her parents, go to rescue her. Her parents entreat in unison, "Come down to us, my child," calling, "do not destroy your life; you will kill us, we have no child but you." The daughter makes a brief farewell speech:

> You have forced me to leave you. I was always a good daughter, and never disobeyed you; and could I have married the man I love, I should have been happy, and would never have left you. But you have been cruel to me; you turned my beloved from the wigwam; you would have forced me to marry a man I hated; I go to the house of the spirits.[44]

In Sommerville's version, Oola-Ita's father leads

the hunters in an attempt to save her, but they arrive too late for dialogue or speeches. As the action unfolds, Sommerville carefully details the setting and thought process of the maiden. The final scene takes place at night, with the moon rising against a backdrop of cliffs. Oola-Ita wonders briefly about life after death, and whether the great spirit will be pleased that she remained true to her lover. As she hears the rescuers approach, the scene switches to the father's grief. Oola-Ita's choice reflects Sommerville's personal concept of duty, honor to a sacred vow.

His interest in human nature is also apparent in "Some Remarks on Hand-Shaking," published the following October.[45] Here he writes a satire on a commonplace human gesture: the handshake. The essay opens with a dry understatement characteristic of Sommerville's wit: "Today is peculiarly the day of science; there is a science for moving, sleeping, and even murder has been reduced to a fine art."[46] Continuing the satire, he casts aside the scientific method, and begins an extended definition of a handshake. He first asks why people shake hands, speculates about the origin of the gesture, and proceeds to classify handshakers in two groups: ones with whom a handshake is pleasant, and ones with whom a handshake is unpleasant.

Among the latter, the most disagreeable are the "hand-crushing" variety, whose grip is so powerful that it inflicts pain. This group also includes men who subject the hearer to long-winded reminiscences, all the while pumping the listener's hand up and down, perhaps to punctuate the discourse. However, the worst, says Sommerville, is the "jocular bore" who, after a polite handshake, subjects his victim to a long and tedious oration.

By contrast, the kind of handshake most men would cherish is a greeting from an old friend or close relative. Here Sommerville displays his versatility as a writer, ranging from satire to sentiment, as he creates a scene at the bedside of his dying mother: "How thin and shadowy was her hand, as it lay upon her breast! How light it felt when you took it in yours! She couldn't press yours much—she was too weak then—but little as it was you felt that pressure, nor have you ceased to feel it yet."[47]

Although Sommerville did not choose to become a fiction writer and essayist, he might well have developed his skills in these areas. His ability to describe landscapes and use emotional appeal was not common in the writings of his contemporaries in *The Hampden-Sidney Magazine.* His personal values, interest in nature and dramatic effects would later enhance his teaching and his hobbies of acting and painting. As well, his youthful essays remain models of erudition, style, and wit for later generations of students to enjoy.

Notes

1. *Catalogue of the Officers and Students of Hampden-Sidney* (1891), 1.

2. Ibid., 6.

3. Many of Sommerville's school mates went on to lead notable lives. John Maxwell Robeson became rector of St. Paul's Episcopal Church in Lynchburg, Virginia. Between the time that they renewed their acquaintance in the same town, Robeson served as a chaplain and saw action on the Texas Border Patrol in 1916-17, served in France during World War I seeing extensive fighting in the Battles of Ypres, Flanders, in the Somme Offensive, and was wounded in Roisell, France. After being sent state-side, he continued serving as a military chaplain until his discharge. (See biographical sketch in the (1924) *History of Virginia 5*, 97)

A.J. Morrison graduated in 1895 and shared membership in the Philanthropic Society and worked on the literary magazines along with Sommerville. He became a noted author and authority on

Colonial Virginia and on the history of Hampden-Sydney and its presidents. Although he received his Ph.D. in Romance Languages from John's Hopkins and taught off and on, he preferred to be a farmer and to spend his free time as a researcher and writer. He was a prolific writer with an interesting pedigree; his paternal grandfather was the founder and first president of Davidson College, his maternal grandfather had been a president of Hampden-Sydney and his mother was a matron of the then State Normal School for Women in Longwood, now known as Longwood College. (See biographical Sketch in *History of Virginia 6,* 171-172)

Henry Irving Brock who succeeded "Rich" as editor of *The Magazine*, went on to become an associate editor of the *New York Times Saturday Magazine*. His father, Henry Clay Brock was Richard's French and Latin professor and his brother, Robert Kincaid Brock, who graduated in 1897, became a state senator, representing the twenty-eighth district of Virginia. (See biographical sketch of the Brock Family in *The History of Virginia 5*, 149)

Other classmates included Richard Lee Morton who was head of the history department of William and Mary, and a noted authority on Virginia history as well as the South specializing in the Civil War and the years that followed; H.B. Arbuckle became head of the chemistry department of Davidson College and J. Layton Mauze, who was probably a distant relative, was a noted Presbyterian minister and leader of the Presbyterian churches of the South.

4. Ibid., *Catalogue* (1891), 33.

5. A copy of his application is found within the Welton Family papers.

6. Ibid., *Catalogue* (1891), 1-35.

7. Ibid., (1895), 6.

8. Ibid., (1894 and 1895), passim.

9. Rand B. Evans, "The Origins in American Academic Psychology," in J. Brožek, Ed., *Explorations in the History of Psychology in the United States.* (Lewisburg: Bucknell Press, 1984), 32-33.

10. Samuel Stanhope Smith, *The Lectures, Corrected and Improved, Which Have Been Delivered for a Series of Years, in the College of New Jersey; on the Subjects of Moral and Political*

Philosophy (Trenton, N.J.: Daniel Fenton, 1812), 13., quoted by Evans, in Brožek, 33.

11. Noah Porter was a professor of moral philosophy and metaphysics at Yale. *The Elements of Moral Science* combined ethical considerations and psychological topics within the context of moral philosophy, but more importantly, psychology was being introduced into the curriculum.

12. *Catalogue of the Officers and Students of Hampden-Sidney* (1895), 33.

13. *Y.M.C.A. Hand-book* (1894), 8.

14. John Sinclair Watt, "History of the Philanthropic Society" (Unpublished and Undated), 1-6.

15. A. M. Fauntleroy, M.D., *The Record of Hampden-Sydney Alumni Association 4* (January 1930): 12.

16. *The Minutes of the Philanthropic Society 2 (1885-1891):* 9.

17. Ibid., 19.

18. Ibid., 21-28.

19. Ibid., 60, 80, 82, 220.

20. Ibid., 220.

21. F.W. Shepardson, *The Story of Beta Theta Pi* (Wisconsin: The Collegiate Press, George Banta Publishing Co., 1930), 462.

22. *The Student's Hand-book 2* (1895), 10.

23. R.G. See, "The Last Comrade," *The Record of Hampden-Sydney 44 and 45* (1970-71):16.

24. *Y.M.C.A. Hand-Book* (1894), 44.

25. Ibid., 5

26. Additional references used in creating the composite of student life and information re R.C. Sommerville:

— The Welton Family Papers.

— Interviews with Ms. Virginia Redd and Professor John Brinkley.

— *The Catalogue, Hampden-Sidney College 27 (1896)*, 42-44. (1987), 9.

— *Student's Register 1849-1905* Hampden-Sydney Archives.

27. Sommerville's family was fond of tennis and crocket.

28. *The Hampden-Sidney Magazine* (1894): 354-355.

29. Richard Clarke Sommerville, "Editorial," *The Hampden-Sidney Magazine*, 13 1 (October 1895): 22.

30. Ibid., 2 (November 1895): 55.

31. The newspaper clipping was found within the Welton Family Papers.

32. Robert L. Scribner, "'In Memory of Frank Padget': Did Virginians Ever Erect Monuments to Honor Negro Slaves? This is the Story of One Who Did" *Virginia Cavalcade*, 3, 3 (Winter 1953): 11. The curious punctuation is as shown in Scribner's photograph and transcription of the inscription on the monument.

33. Richard Clarke Sommerville, "The Slave-Hero," *The Hampden-Sidney Magazine 12*, 3 (December 1894): 85-91.

34. The curriculum at Hampden-Sydney clearly demonstrates that in Sommerville's time, students were expected to receive moral edification from their studies of oratory, composition, and literature. This tradition was derived from classical Greek and Roman educational models, and was handed down through the works of authors like Aristotle, Cicero, and Quintilian.

35. Sommerville, "The Slave-Hero," (1894): 86.

36. Ibid.

37. Ibid., 87.

38. Ibid., 87-88.

39. Richard Clarke Sommerville, "As a Man Thinketh," *The Prism*, (February 1940): 16.

40. Richard Clarke Sommerville, "Oola-Ita," *The Hampden-Sidney Magazine 11*, 6 (1894): 310-314.

41. *Dahcohtah; or Life and Legends of the Sioux around Fort Snelling*. Preface by C. M. Kirkland (New York: John Wiley, 1849), 165-173. Eastman does observe that this legend was popular among the Sioux, and that many versions of it circulated during her time. Although various tribes were credited with its origins, she learned of it from the Dakota (Sioux) Indians living around Fort Snelling, MN. By 1894, Helen Hunt Jackson had published her novel *Ramona*, a derivative of this legend in which a young Indian woman, unable to be united with her lover, leaps to her death from a cliff. In the late nineteenth century, "Lover's Leaps" began appearing in various parts of the United States. "Indian Love Call," the maiden's parting song, was being performed at Indian ceremonials for tourists. See *Literature by and about the American Indian: An Annotated Bibliography*. Ed. Anna Lee Stensland and Aune M. Fadum. 2nd ed. (Urbana: National Council of Teachers of English, 1979), 15-16.

SGCCC LIBRARY
WITHDRAWN
4601 Mid Rivers Mall Drive
St. Peters, MO 63376

42. Sommerville, "Oola-Ita," (1894): 310.

43. For a nineteenth-century drawing of this location, see Eastman, *Dahcohtah*, 165. The 1943 *Collier's World Atlas and Gazetteer* locates a "Maiden Rock" on the eastern shore of the lake. Recent atlases do not show this point.

44. Eastman, 168.

45. Richard Clarke Sommerville, "Some Remarks on Hand-Shaking," *The Hampden-Sidney Magazine* 12, 1(October 1894): 15-20.

46. Ibid., 15.

47. Ibid., 20. Here he would have to be imagining, because his own mother was still alive; she died in 1912.

3

THE RESTLESS YOUNG MAN

The years following graduation from Hampden-Sydney were filled with travel, teaching, studying, and some adventure. Sommerville put down few roots before the age of fifty. For the next thirty years of his life, he was to be a restless man, moving around the country frequently as his travels were to take him to places far away from his native Virginia.

Richard's teaching career began in September of 1896 at Hardin Institute located in Elizabethtown, Kentucky, where he taught Latin and mathematics. His stay there lasted only one year. In September of 1897, he moved to Broaddus Institute in Clarksburg, West Virginia, where he served as the boys' principal and taught science and mathematics.[1] Richard's stay in Clarksburg was also one year.

The Teacher Becomes a Beggar and Jailor

During the winter at Clarksburg, Sommerville became ill and appeared unable to recover. In early June of

1898, he went to his home in Moorefield. While the "Social Page" of *The Hardy County News* announced on July 17, 1898 that he was in town visiting his family for several weeks, he was seriously ill. His family was convinced that he had "consumption," for which the only known cure was to seek the warmer and drier climate of the Arizona Territories. According to Dr. Felix Welton, his nephew, the prescriptive treatment for tuberculosis in those days was to sleep on the desert floor. Young Richard was sent out West to die. Later in life, he confided that he resented being sent away, and on several occasions, he even doubted that he ever had tuberculosis, but he did.

On his résumé, Sommerville simply explained away the two years of his life without working as "two years of travel." Leaving in the summer of 1898, he went to Texas, Arizona, and parts of California. While in the desert, he enjoyed the cacti and fauna but disliked the tumbleweed. Later he was to tell of a trip to the Grand Canyon: traveling with a German photographer from Flagstaff, an Irishman who liked to sing, and an American who painted, they found an old log cabin late one day where they sought shelter for the night. The following morning he arose early and made his way to the rim of the Grand Canyon which was filled with mist. When the sun came up, little by little, the mist went away, and the sight was revealed to him gradually, now here and then there. The colors of the sunrise added to the spectacle, and Sommerville felt this was the most beautiful sight that he had ever seen. He returned every morning of his stay there to relive this pageantry of nature. This trip also included a visit to the foot of the Cataract Canyon where he met and stayed with a tribe of Indians for a week.[2]

A second visual experience occurred during a visit to the San Francisco Mountains in Northern Arizona. Sommerville saw sparks leaping from the peaks, a phenomenon caused by static electricity. He later learned that these sparks were quite dangerous.

While living in Arizona, Sommerville had no funds, and he later told stories of near starvation. He told of eating prairie onions which made him ill, of attempting to hunt prairie dogs without success, and of begging some horse corn from a livery stable and roasting it over an open fire. He also learned to locate edible plants and make a loaf of bread last three or four days.

Sometime during 1899 or the winter of 1900, Richard took a job as a bookkeeper in the sheriff's office in Flagstaff, Arizona. As he knew nothing about keeping records when he took the job on a Friday, over the weekend, he bought a book on how to do bookkeeping, and reported to work the following Monday.[3] He functioned more as a deputy than a bookkeeper because the sheriff was committed to an "insane asylum," and the regular deputy liked to spend time in the gambling saloons. Consequently, along with his regular duties, Richard had to get food for the prisoners and guard them. According to one source:

> Because of the sheriff's absence and the deputy's other duties, Dr. Sommerville found that his duties included more than keeping books, but also the prisoners. In order to feed the bunch he had to unlock the cells and allow the prisoners, one a murderer, into a common room where they ate. Although he carried a .44 while performing this duty, he did not neglect making friends with the prisoners. This paid dividends for one day during the meal time one of the prisoners, who was new to the group announced that he was leaving. The old prisoners stood between the new prisoner and the door causing him to change his mind on the matter saving Sommerville a good deal of trouble.[4]

To this day, oral history about Sommerville's life in the old West, includes some interesting stories. Some said that he had chased Indians and went out on sheriff's posses; others allowed that he had stopped a jail-break. Efforts to learn more about the many stories concerning his "deputy-sheriff days out West," have met with mixed results. A brief note in *The Weekly Gem*, Flagstaff, Arizona, on August 24, 1899 announced the appointment of a new sheriff of Coconino County "occasioned by the insanity of Fletcher Fairchild."[5] Likewise, the May 20, 1899 minutes, recorded in *The Great Register* (Flagstaff, Arizona), show that Sheriff Fairchild was granted a ninety-day leave-of-absence, and on August 18, a physician certified before town council that Sheriff Fairchild was insane. Bonnie Greer of the Arizona Historical Society spent countless hours researching the existing records of the sheriff's office and the minutes of the town council. No mention is made of Richard Clarke Sommerville, not even that he registered to vote.[6]

As the records are not complete, and it is not certain exactly when Richard Sommerville worked as a book-keeper, his experiences out West remain somewhat mysterious. However, it is unlikely that he went out on posses or chased Indians as some of the folklore would have it. The primary reason to believe that he worked as a book-keeper is that he said he did, but nowhere does he recount in any of the many interviews anything other than the experiences he encountered as a jailer. Although he had a keen interest in native American culture, those interests were academic. But the story that he was one of the few "deputies" who could read and write, much less have a master's degree in the classics, probably stands!

The Teacher Returns to the Classroom

Fully restored to health and ready to resume his teaching career, Sommerville returned to Moorefield in the summer of 1900. The following September, he taught English and history at the Shenandoah Valley Academy for Boys which was located in Winchester, Virginia. According to James Somerville, his nephew, while he was there for one year, he taught Thomas, Richard, and Harry Byrd, the future United States Senator from Virginia.[7]

Again feeling the need to move on, in the summer of 1901, Sommerville moved to Savannah, Georgia, to teach Latin and science at Morton's School for Boys. Morton's School was probably both a primary and a secondary school. From time to time, an advertisement announcing the acceptance of applications by students appeared in *The Savannah Morning News* and the Sunday, March 8, 1903 edition ran the following:

Morton's School for Boys
13-17 East Macon
"Prepares for College; fit for business"
J.R. Morton, M.A. Principal R.C. Sommerville, M.A. First Assist.
R.E.L. Farmer, M.A. Principal Miss Edith Johnson, Second Assist.[8]

Richard taught at this boys' school for five years in subjects ranging from Latin to the sciences. In the summer of 1904, he took time off to attend a summer course in Latin for Teachers at Harvard University.

Not content to work for others at this juncture in his life, Sommerville decided to follow the model of his sisters and open his own school. In 1905, he opened a school for boys located at 808 Drayton Street in Savannah, apparently taking over a school previously advertised as the Savannah Academy for Boys. The June 7 and 9, 1905 editions of *The Savannah Morning News* carry the following announcement:

Mr. R.C. Somerville (sic) announces that in Oct. 1905, he will open a School for Boys at 808 Drayton St. The many new

and attractive features which will be introduced into this school
will, he hopes, make it worthy of the patronage of his friends
and the careful consideration of all parents.[9]

During the years from 1900 through approximately
1906, most of the newspaper coverage about education
included the private schools. The Sommerville School
became a competitor to Morton's School for Boys, which
was now located at 111 Park Avenue West, as well as to the
Savannah Preparatory School.[10] These schools actively
competed with one another in the newspapers with Morton's
School for Boys advertising that its graduates could get
into schools, such as Hampden-Sydney, the University of
Virginia, the University of Georgia, and William and
Mary, among others, without entrance exams.[11] The advertisements for the Savannah Preparatory School stated that
it was the only school fully accredited by the state examiner. The Savannah Academy for Boys also advertised a
summer camp for boys (which Sommerville continued to
operate). In the June 13 and 15 editions of the newspaper,
and subsequently, every four to seven days thereafter
through December of 1905, larger advertisements for the
Sommerville School appear, for example:

The Sommerville School
808 Drayton St.
Central Location-Thorough Instruction
Attractive Interior, Library and Social Room
Well Equipped Gymnasium
Catalogue may be had in the book stores
or will be mailed upon request.[12]

The Sommerville School was closed in 1910 without formal announcement. Although one story surfaced
that the school burned, the more probable reason for the
school's closing was Sommerville's health. His *Vita* lists

one year of rest for 1910-1911, which is how he typically referenced his illness.

It is certain, however, that in addition to competing with each other, these private, mostly classical schools were now competing with the public schools of Savannah. At the turn of the century, the public schools were scarcely mentioned in the papers. By 1910 and 1911, they were getting much newspaper coverage as, in the state of Georgia, there was much enthusiasm for public education, This enthusiasm was beginning to spread across the nation. Public education, however, was of no interest to Richard Sommerville.

The Teacher is also a Hussar

The eleven years that Sommerville lived in Savannah, Georgia, were longer than he had stayed in any other place since his birth. Teaching school was not his only interest. For recreation and adventure, he joined the Hussars National Guard, the Calvary Division. According to Lindsey P. Henderson, Jr., a noted historian of the Georgia Hussars, Sommerville was admitted to membership on November 13, 1902 and retired on November 19, 1906.[13] Membership in the Hussars was no small investment. Each member was required to furnish his own horse, uniform, arms, and equipment. After the Civil War and before World War II, all of the activities were mostly ceremonial for this unit. Sommerville loved the ceremony and took part proudly dressed in his bright red uniform with the plumb on the hat. At his side was his sabre which he mastered as he was a prize winning fencer in competition.

All events involving the military units of Savannah were routinely carried in the Savannah newspapers. Members of the National Guard received their "call-up"

Richard Sommerville In Hussars Dress, 1904
(Courtesy of Mrs. Felix Welton)

orders through the classified advertisement sections of the local newspapers. These orders were typically marked with an emblem of a Hussar astride a horse and were located in the upper right hand corner of the notice. The Hussars were a proud tradition in Savannah and provided the town with entertainment. Every year on the anniversary of Robert E. Lee's birthday, a parade marking the occasion was held in Savannah. Sommerville would have been proud to participate. He told William Shackelford, his student and later good friend, that Lee was one of his heroes and that he admired him for his sense of commitment to duty. The Monday, January 19, 1903 edition of *The Savannah Morning News* carries a front-page description of one such parade:

> The rear was brought up by the Georgia Hussars under command of Capt. W.W. Jordan, Jr.. The tramp of the hoof, champ of the bit and clank of the sabre, combined with the handsome uniform, and the large plumb which waved defiantly in the breeze, lent to the command a most pleasing, and at once war-like appearance....[14]

After the parade, the newspaper account went on to say that the Hussars stayed at the drill grounds and "engaged in difficult drill movements." This parade was a major annual event for the community, and most of the citizens turned out in celebration. Other newspaper accounts told of how the Hussars participated in ceremonial rites from time to time and marveled often at the complexities of the sabre drills. Clearly this was an exciting spectacle, and the large turnouts by spectators gave Sommerville an opportunity to demonstrate his flair for the dramatic. In later years, he liked to admit that he was quite a *beau sabre*. Certainly it could have been a reminder of his youth in Moorefield observing the jousting tournaments and dreaming of knights of old.

In 1906, at the age of thirty-one, Sommerville left
the Hussars. During the time that he was a member, the
unit's activities were totally ceremonial. However, during 1916-1917, a division was sent to the Texas border
with Mexico and some of its members went on the
punitive raids into Mexico against "Pancho" Villa. During that year, Sommerville was then at Milford, Texas,
employed as the president of the Texas Presbyterian
College for Girls. In later years, stories surfaced that
Sommerville had "chased 'Pancho' Villa over Mexico."
His involvement with the Hussars and his location in
Texas at the time were not the only explanation for the
stories. His nephew, Julian Hatcher, was an artillery
specialist serving with the border patrol with General
Pershing.[15] Richard was very proud of his nephew and
told stories not only about his the adventures in Mexico,
but also in France during World War I. Over the years, the
stories were probably modified giving Sommerville credit
for his nephew's exploits. According to Colonel
Henderson, his uncle, Retired General A. Rester
Henderson, a former Captain of the Hussars who served
on the border in 1916-17, does not remember Sommerville
being there. According to this source, the only forty-
year-olds were two officers whom both gentlemen knew
personally, and neither was a Sommerville.

The Teacher Becomes a President

Although Richard's health, in part, contributed to
the closing of his school and, for the second time, interrupted his teaching career, he always managed to recover
and move onward. In August of 1911, Sommerville became president of the Lewisburg Female Institute and
Seminary located in Lewisburg, West Virginia.

In a letter to the editor of *The Greenbrier Independent* on Thursday, August 3, 1911, Reverend Ben Harrop, president of the Greenbrier Presbytery, announced Sommerville's appointment. Included in the announcement were verbatim quotes from his references (all of which referred to the position of principal, but Sommerville's title was president) which are the only extant information concerning The Sommerville School for Boys.
According to the announcement:

> Mr. Sommerville comes to us most highly commended as a christian gentleman and teacher in every sense, as may be seen from the following extracts from letters:
> From W.W. Owens, M.D., Savannah, Ga., 'Replying to your favor enquiring as to the fitness of Mr. R.C. Sommerville for the position of principal of your school, I beg to say that I can and so most heartily recommend him in every way. My own son was under him in his school in this city for three years and his teaching of him was of the highest order. Mr. Sommerville is a high-toned, gentlemanly scholar in every sense of the word.'
> From Rev. W. Moore Scott, Pastor of First Presbyterian Church, Savannah, Ga. and President of Board of Presbyterial Institute of Savannah Presbytery: 'Replying to your enquiry concerning Mr. R.C. Sommerville. will (sic) say that his school here was a marked success and it had a large future and enviable reputation assured. I made the address to the students at the closing exercises one year and was, a time or two, more in position to observe the school and it made a splendid impression upon me—especially the high grade of teachers and the first-class appearance of everything in general. My impressions are so favorable that were he available for consideration by our school, as I occupy the same position as I believe you do from the communication I received. I (sic) should consider him before any one else.'
> From Walter Hallihen, professor of the Greek in the University of the South: 'Replying to your enquiry in regard to the qualifications of Mr. R.C. Sommerville for the position of principal of the Lewisburg Female Seminary, it gives me great pleasure to say that I think you would be indeed fortunate if you

can secure him for this position. Mr. Sommerville taught in my summer camp for three or four years and out of perhaps a hundred men who have taught for me for the past twelve years I should rate him among the five best teachers. He possesses a pleasing address and has a very dignified bearing. He is a man who is thoroughly conscientious and in every sense a gentleman. I repeat that the Seminary will be fortunate to secure him and I have little doubt of its success under his administration.'[16]

The themes found within his references—high-toned gentleman, scholar, dignified bearing, one of the best teachers, conscientious—were the themes associated with Richard Sommerville certainly by the end of his teaching career. These references, written when he was in his late twenties and early thirties, indicate that these distinguishing qualities formed early. That his school was highly regarded is also apparent within the letters of recommendation.

Changing its name several times, The Lewisburg Seminary for Girls was originally called the Lewisburg Academy when founded in 1812. In 1874, the name was changed to the Lewisburg Female Institute. In 1911, just before Sommerville arrived, the name was again changed to the Lewisburg Seminary and came under the control of the Greenbrier Presbytery.[17] Later the school became known as Greenbrier College and was an independent private junior college for women. The school closed permanently after the 1970-71 school year.

The school *Catalogue* for 1911-12 showed that 110 students were enrolled, ranging in ages between seven and twenty years. Several students over the age of twenty were listed as special students in music, including Richard's youngest sister, Sophie White Sommerville, a special student of piano. Her primary position, according to *The Greenbrier Independent*, was as a clerk and stenographer for her brother.[18]

Three programs were offered at the school: an elementary school program, a high school diploma program, and a program in music education. The *Catalogue* stated clearly that the seminary was "not a college" but a school designed to educate young women to become "useful citizens."[19] The curriculum overlapped with that of Hampden-Sydney, not only in the use of certain texts at the higher levels, such as Latin, English, mathematics, and science, but also in the study of moral philosophy during the last two years. All young women, regardless of their program of study, had to first enroll in a course in psychology and then a course in ethics. The specified textbooks included Peabody's *Manual of Moral Philosophy, the Classical Course*, and Davis' *Elements of Ethics*, followed by John Dewey's *Moral Principles of Education*. The course description for moral philosophy indicated that the issues of concern included the nature of desire and motives, with significance placed on the "interpretation of human freedom," and the study of moral standards and virtue. The school's philosophy for the education of young ladies at the Lewisburg Seminary was stated quite clearly just as it had been for the young men at Hampden-Sydney. A common theme, the purpose of education, was to train the mind through the lecture and recitation classes at the elementary level. For the higher grades, this basic education served as the foundation for contemplating the responsibilities inherit in personal choices, and for studying values of culture as they pertain to freedom, duty, and social obligations.

When Richard was hired, the school enrollment was on the decline, and the school was heavily in debt. His job was to work with a special committee of the board to help retire the debt which had accrued mainly because of an extensive refurbishing of buildings and the purchase of new equipment.[20] He proved himself in every way to the

board and to the town as indicated by the newspaper after
two months on the job.

> Prof. Sommerville impresses all as the right man in the place
> to which he has been chosen. He is giving close attention to
> every detail in the management of the school, the classification
> of students, and the work of the schoolroom and the discipline
> he has already established meets the hearty approval of his
> assistants and the patrons of the school here. All feel confident
> that he will 'make good' and that the results of his discipline and
> his careful supervision of the work done in the schoolroom will
> make manifest the wisdom of the Board of Directors in electing
> him as head of the school.[21]

Richard Sommerville's first year as president of
the school was quite successful as indicated by the local
newspaper which closely followed the activities, not
only at the seminary, but also at the nearby Greenbrier
Military School for boys. Felix Welton, a student at the
seminary, lived with "Uncle Rich" for one year in the
president's home before moving to the Greenbrier Military School. Dr. Welton described his uncle as a strict
but patient president who attended to every detail.
Every Saturday, he went along with his uncle to inspect
the dormitories. This inspection was to check for neat-
ness on the part of the students as well as to keep up with
needed repairs. Fires were a constant threat in those
days and therefore fire inspections were a necessary
routine. Should anything need improvement or repair, it
had to be done the following week and before the next
inspection. Should any student not have her room as
neat as he expected, he would ask her if she could do
better next time. His style was never to reproach the
student, but to make suggestions for improvements. He
said that "Uncle Rich" never really had trouble with
discipline because he projected an air of expectation for
good behavior, and he usually got it.

Dr. Welton enjoyed living with his uncle and had the opportunity to watch him work and to get to know him very well. He recalled that Richard was always neat and kept things tidy, but also he never threw anything away. He remembered a large walk-in closet used not only for clothes, but for the storage of hundreds of cigar boxes. Occasionally he stored some things in them, but he had many extras.[22] He also kept all the wooden button-covers which were used by the local laundry to protect shirt buttons during washing. When making out teaching schedules, his living room was cluttered with these buttons as he flagged them in some uniform way, moving them around while attempting to ensure no scheduling conflicts among the teachers.

Sommerville was an enormously popular president of the Lewisburg Seminary. The newspaper recorded his daily activities. Even the content of his talks, lectures, and the occasional talk given at the Old Stone Presbyterian Church were not only recounted, but editorialized. As one of the leading citizens of the town, in May of 1913, Sommerville had the opportunity to escort the Vice-President of the United States, Thomas R. Marshall, who had been invited to help celebrate the seventy-fifth anniversary of the organization of the Greenbrier Presbytery and the one-hundredth session of the schools. Sommerville served as one of the two official escorts for Vice-President Marshall and as the master of ceremonies for several of the formal events.[23]

By 1916, he had increased the enrollment in the school, had provided scholarships for the young ladies to study based on merit, and now employed some fifteen faculty members. However, his health would not permit him to stay. On May 9, 1916, the newspaper carried the announcement that Sommerville was resigning to take a similar position at the Texas Presbyterian College for Girls at Milford, Texas. Sorrow was expressed in losing his services and the paper stated:

> ...He has served the school here most acceptably and will leave Lewisburg with the highest respect, good opinion and best wishes of us all. He has managed the affairs of the school carefully and systematically, always submitting model reports to the board, has maintained good discipline, kept in close touch with every department of the work and held at all times the respect and confidence of the teachers, patrons and pupils.[24]

A later account said that he had resigned because of his health and that he needed to seek a warmer climate. This edition also recounted the formal farewell to Sommerville, saying that he "did not attempt to make a farewell address merely remarking that there are times when the heart is too full and emotions too deep for utterance."[25]

For the second time in his life, Richard's health problems forced him to leave a situation that he enjoyed and head south. This was the third time that his health interrupted his teaching career. He must have been very disappointed because he hated to be sick, and moreover, he had been in Texas before and he did not like the place.

Richard Sommerville was the second president in the history of the Texas Presbyterian College for Girls (now Austin College and located in Sherman, Texas), succeeding Dr. Henry Clay Evans, a Presbyterian minister who had helped to found the school. There was much optimism about his appointment in the press announcement of March 25, 1916. Parents and patrons of the school were told that Sommerville had come to them with "recommendations of the first order as an instructor, administrator, and disciplinarian," and the accounts described him as a "cultured, refined, Christian gentle-man."[26] He arrived early in the summer to help with new preparations for the college program in the fall. The preparations referred to included the addition of a new program in domestic science which was being added to the curriculum.

The school was billed as a junior college and as a liberal arts college leading to the B.A. with three tracks for the women to pursue:

> First, a standard high-school course, which is sufficient to admit to the best woman's college. Second, a seminary course, which embraces all of the first course, and, in addition, an extra year's drill which is the full equivalent of regular college freshman work; this for students who wish to complete their education here. Third, for those expecting to teach, a normal course, which will entitle the graduate to a State certificate.[27]

As can be seen from the above description, this school departed somewhat from the other schools in Sommerville's past because there were now two applied studies programs, one leading to a state teacher's license and the other in domestic science. The curriculum at this Texas school was reflective of the changes that were beginning to take shape at that time. Applied studies were becoming acceptable within the liberal studies curriculum. The pure classical studies with an emphasis on Latin, Greek, and mathematics were gradually being replaced, not only with modern languages, but also by practical career training.

Sommerville was to stay less than eighteen months, long enough to complete the introduction of the domestic science program. World War I was underway and he decided to "do his part." He abruptly resigned in 1918.

The Teacher Reports for War Duty

In the spring of 1918, Richard Sommerville reported to the Edgewood Arsenal to work with the Young

Men's Christian Association (Y.M.C.A.) War Works Program. A 1918 newspaper clipping announced the change in the presidency saying that Dr. Henry Clay Evans, the first president of the school, would return because Sommerville was going to join the Y.M.C.A. program in France.[28]

This program, which was begun during the Civil War by the Y.M.C.A, was expanded after the Spanish American War of 1898. It included the development of physical facilities which were built on or near the grounds of army and navy bases. Two hundred and ninety such buildings constructed by the Y.M.C.A. between 1900 and 1916. They provided for "free corresponding materials, ice water to discourage beer drinking at the army canteens, newspapers and magazines, a pamphlet of *Medical Rules for Camp Life*, [and] indoor and outdoor games."[29] Religious programs, evangelical and revivalistic in nature were central. Song books, Bibles, and Testaments were prepared and distributed by the thousands. The goal of this program was to provide a "home away from home for the soldier and sailor."[30] Among the activities were social programs, lectures, entertainment, and church parties. Religious work was strongly emphasized. Additionally, the ill, and during war-time, the wounded, were visited in hospital. Physical fitness and team sports were emphasized.

Although one might think it unusual for a man of forty-three to resign from a rather prestigious and safe position to volunteer for such a potentially dangerous program, four factors probably came to bear on his decision. First, he was indeed patriotic and felt a certain duty. He once said that he was too old for the military but could serve his country by working with the Y program. Secondly, he did not like Texas. He told his nephew that he could not bear to have his windows constantly caked with sand. Thirdly, he was probably contacted and asked to serve. Fourthly, he loved change and new challenges.

Providing services to the troop trains, the Y.M.C.A. operated the canteens in France during World War I. The program also operated leave centers at resort areas, helped with the deployment of services and staff major offenses, worked in occupied Germany, and helped to transport troops back to their respective countries. In the beginning when the planning was underway, the members were unaware of the colossal job which lay ahead. About 25,926 persons actually served the Y during this time in the United States, Russia, The British Isles, Poland, and in occupied Germany. However, these were not enough. The organization called on its membership to offer both time and money, and they were successful.[31]

Planning to go to France, Sommerville went to the Edgewood Arsenal, one of five established during World War I, but the Armistice was signed before he was shipped out. He once told a student that he held the rank of officer, and that his duties were to minister to the spiritual and physical needs of the wounded soldiers.[32] His brother, Charles, was the Y.M.C.A. Chaplain at Parris Island at the same time.

Sommerville's long-standing association with the Y.M.C.A., dating back to his college days at Hampden-Sydney, placed him right for the call. His intense sense of loyalty to his country, his often publicly stated belief that the free had a moral obligation to fight for the freedom of others, were sufficient to compel him from safety into potential peril. This was also the first time in international conflict that he was well enough to volunteer. During the Spanish-American War, he was in the West foraging for food. He was, however, part of the generations of Americans, beginning at the turn of the century, who thought of the United States as the growing leader of the world. They thought that the United States not only could, but should promote democracy in every country throughout the world. Following the War, Sommerville worked briefly for the Red Cross in New York City, and apparently was at loose ends for a time. He was contemplating the remainder of his life and what he wanted to do with it. He did not want to go back into elementary and secondary education, and began to consider teaching at the college and university level where there were growing opportunities. After much reflection, he decided to return to school for doctoral studies in psychology, and he chose Columbia University.

Notes

1. The Broaddus Institute was a Baptist college and was originally established in 1871 in Winchester, Virginia. Five years later it was moved to Clarksburg, West Virginia where today it is still a private four-year liberal arts school. Frederic Morton, *The Story of Winchester in Virginia (1776-1861), III,* (Strasburg, Virginia: Shenandoah Publishing House, 1925), 238-9.

2. Mervyn Williamson Papers. Interview and rough draft of article, (undated) Lynchburg College Archives. Uncatalogued.

3. Mervyn Williamson, "Man of Many Parts," *The Lynchburg College Magazine* (1972): 8.

4. Yon Schoenmaker, "Dr. Richard C. Sommerville Relates Varied Events of Unusual Career," *The Critograph* (1953): 5.

5. Bonnie Greer, Letters to author, 15 August and 25 November 1985 with enclosures from *The Weekly Gem* (August 15, September 24, November 25, 1899), Arizona Historical Society, Flagstaff, Arizona.

6. Greer, Researcher, Pioneer Museum, Flagstaff, Arizona. Letter to author, 15 August 1985.

7. James Somerville, *Somerville Family of White Post, Virginia* (unpublished: Welton Family Papers), 16.

8. *The Savannah Morning News (1900-1911),* J. H. Estill, Publishers. Microfilm Publications (Rochester, New York: The Uni-

versity of Rochester Library), 7.

    9. Ibid., 2.

    10. Ibid., 7.

    11. Ibid., (October 8, 1905), 8.

    12. Ibid.

    13. A. Reston Henderson, Letter to author with enclosures, 24 May 1984.

    14. *The Savannah Morning News*, 1.

    15. Julian Hatcher was the eldest son of Ada and Lindley Hatcher. He graduated from Annapolis but transferred to the army where he became a Major-General. At the time of his death, his picture and obituary appeared in *The Washington Post* on Thursday, December, 5, 1963 (Welton Family Papers). He was described as "one of the world's leading experts on small arms" and as an author of books on the subject. As a young Captain in charge of munitions during the Mexican Border Campaign of 1916, he served with General Pershing. He amassed the small arms arsenal and went on the punitive raids against "Pancho" Villa. When Pershing was sent to France in charge of the American forces during World War I, Hatcher was also sent as the munitions expert. Julian was the second of his family to graduate from Annapolis. His great uncle, Ensign Charles Aby, brother to Maria Sommerville, was a member of the first graduating class from Annapolis. This uncle was credited by Sommerville as inspiring his hobby of building model sailboats as a child.

    16. *The Greenbrier Independent* 46 6 (August 3, 1911): 3 c2. Microfilm Publications, (1909-1917), Charleston: The State of West Virginia Archives.

    17. *Annual Reports of the Executive Committee of Christian Education and Ministerial Relief of the Presbyterian Church in the U.S.* (1936), 14. The Historical Foundation of the Presbyterian and Reformed Churches, Inc. Montreat, North Carolina.

    18. *The Greenbrier Independent*, 46 (September 4, 1911): 2, 3, c.4.

    19. *The Catalogue*, Lewisburg Seminary for Girls 1913-1914. (The Historical Foundation of the Presbyterian and Reformed Churches, Inc., Montreat, North Carolina), 33.

    20. *The Greenbrier Independent*, 45, 50 (June 8, 1911): 3 c.

4; *46*, 3 (September 21, 1911): 3, c.6; *46*, 23 (Nov. 30, 1911): 2 c.2.

21. Ibid., *46*, 13 (Sept. 21, 1911): 3, c.6.

22. Richard Sommerville was a cigar smoker all his life and had a tendency to keep all the old cigar boxes in case he needed to store things. At the time of his death, his attic was full of empty boxes, estimated to be in the hundreds. (Mr. George Adams, interview with author, June, 1983).

23. *The Greenbrier Independent*, *47*, 46 (May 8, 1913): 4, c. 1-2.

24. Ibid., *50*, 37: 5.

25. Ibid., *50*, 50 (June 2, 1916): 5.

26. Margaret Hynds, Archivist. Letter to author, 26 August 1985. Summary of newspaper accounts: *The Milford News;* (August 26, 1916). *Texas Presbyterian College Bulletin, I*, 3 (March 1, 1917) and various other undated accounts. Sherman Texas: Austin College Archives.

27. *Texas Presbyterian College Bulletin 1916-17*, 19.

28. Hynds (1985) op. cit.

29. C. H. Hopkins, *History of the Y.M.C.A. in North America* (New York: Associated Press 1951), 454.

30. Ibid., 55.

31. Ibid., 489ff.

32. Jackson Darst, "Behind That Desk - Richard Clarke Sommerville," *The Prism, 7*, 7 (December 1943): 9, 16.

4

A RETURN TO THE CLASSROOM

Graduate Education Is Changing In America

The history of education at the time, makes clear the reasons for Sommerville's personal dilemma. He was more familiar with classical colleges and the one-curriculum approach to education which emphasized Latin, Greek, mathematics, and moral philosophy. This type of school was fading fast at this juncture of his life. From the late eighteen-eighties onward, elective courses began replacing the fixed curriculum, increasing the number of courses to be taught, and opening the door for the creation of separate academic departments. Even as Sommerville was completing his degree at Hampden-Sydney College, graduate schools emphasizing specific majors and requiring research replaced the traditional fifth year of study leading to the master's degree. This change was forced on American education because many American students were choosing to go abroad for graduate studies, particularly to Austria and Germany, where the newer model had originated. In the eighteen-eighties there were as many graduate students abroad as in the United States.[1]

By the second decade of the twentieth century the newer model had become very successful in the United States. Sommerville was aware of these changes. He could either find a job somewhere teaching within the old model, thus becoming outdated, or he could return to school and become a part of the changing curriculum. Sommerville had a second decision to make. Which subject should he choose as a specialty? Armed with a strong background in many subject areas by formal training and teaching experience, he could have chosen any number of disciplines. His interests and talents were wide-ranging from the sciences, to the arts and the humanities. His major interests, however, tended to be focused within psychology, philosophy, and pedagogy. Psychology had quickly become a recognized discipline in its own right, and in many colleges and universities it was being separated from its mother disciplines of philosophy and physiology. His choice of psychology was a reasoned one because its ranging subject matter allowed Sommerville to integrate the areas of study which most intrigued him. Arguably, the best school for him at the time was Columbia University. Its structure allowed him to satisfy his appetite for cross-disciplinary study while earning a specialized degree.

Richard Earns His Degree the Hard Way

Sommerville worked on his doctorate the hard way by teaching and studying at the same time. Beginning with the spring term and through the summer of 1919, he enrolled at Columbia's Teacher's College in New York City. In the summer of 1920, and every summer thereafter until 1923, he enrolled at Columbia University in the

Faculties of Political Science, Philosophy, and Pure Science Division where the program in psychology was housed.[2] In the fall of 1919, he accepted a position at Arkansas College in Batesville, Arkansas, where he taught mental philosophy, ethics, and French. Teaching full-time while being a student is difficult enough, but teaching three different subjects, and studying in a fourth (experimental psychology) was an ambitious undertaking by any standard. This arrangement was necessary because Sommerville was not wealthy, and it allowed him to pay his bills and to work toward his doctorate at the same time. Richard taught full time at Arkansas College, a private liberal arts college, from 1919 through the academic term of 1923. He resigned his teaching post at the end of the 1922-23 term so that he could spend the required year in residence at Columbia University.

Returning full-time at Columbia for the 1923-24 academic year, Sommerville finished his course work and started collecting data for his dissertation. Transcripts from the Office of Information Services, Columbia University, show that he enrolled in five hours of course work including two in statistics and two in research. He received the grade of "A" in statistics and a "P" for the research course.[3] The latter grade was most probably credit showing the completion of his dissertation. The records from Columbia are incomplete, but he stated on his *Vita of Record* that his major was psychology, his minor was education, and that he was enrolled in courses in philosophy.

Columbia's "Golden Age"

Sommerville studied psychology at Columbia University during the era which Frederick C. Thorne called the "Golden Age" (1920-40).[4] According to Thorne, during these years, Columbia University was more of a confederation of undergraduate colleges, graduate programs, professional schools, summer schools, and university extension divisions, with most of these programs running largely independently. Students could take courses of choice throughout the network. At Teacher's College, there was a graduate program in educational psychology with its own doctoral program and courses, and with its own roster of well known faculty. The most noted was John Dewey who was not only affiliated with that program, but also with both the Departments of Psychology and Philosophy at Columbia University's College of Arts and Sciences. Another important figure was Edward Thorndike who, although trained in animal research, had become an educational psychologist. In his own right he influenced education, although somewhat differently from John Dewey who was by far the better known to the general public. Thorndike was highly involved in the development of intelligence testing and created the Thorndike Intelligence Test.

During the time that Sommerville was studying for his doctorate in psychology at Columbia, the school was one of the two major centers (the University of Chicago was the other) associated with the Functionalist movement in the history of psychology. This movement, which had its formal beginnings at the end of the nineteenth century, was the first truly American system within psychology. Its focus was on mental functions as adaptations and adjustments to the environment and reflected the American tendency to be pragmatic and practical in philosophy and in science. The major emphasis was not on what *is* the mind or what *is* the conscious, but how does each *function*. The range of interests for research was broad and included studies from sensory and physical reflexes, to memory systems, to religious experiences, to pedagogy, to intelligence, to the study of abnormal behavior. The behavior of children, young and older adults, as well as animals, was considered as an appropriate area of study. The subject matter of psychology was expanded to include the study of all forms of mental functions which could be defined and measured. The Functionalists adopted a biological tradition and were strongly influenced by Darwinian biology with its emphasis on adaptation to the environment, and the study of individual differences.

Of interest was the organic model of evolution which emphasized the fluid nature of development. Early thinkers and writers on this subject, such as William James of Harvard and John Dewey of Chicago and Columbia, were forerunners of the Functionalist movement; they were two of Sommerville's favorite philosopher-psychologists. Robert Sessions Woodworth, the department chairman until 1925, is credited with being one of the major developers and elaborators of the system.[5] Woodworth taught Richard and served as one of his dissertation advisers from the Department of Psychology.[6]

Woodworth is recognized by some historians of psychology as the dean of American experimental psychology. During his time the program attracted more than an unusual share of gifted and well respected psychologists. It was known for its excellence in teaching and for research, especially for developing what was to become the standard experimental-statistical approach to the study of human and animal behavior. As his dissertation and later research show, Sommerville mastered this approach.

The records at Columbia are incomplete, so no proof exists that Sommerville had enrolled in courses taught by either Dewey or Thorndike. However, according to his *Vita*, he enrolled in enough education courses to have a minor in education at Teacher's College, and he also studied philosophy at Columbia University. It is highly doubtful that Sommerville would have passed up a chance to study with Dewey since he had already used Dewey's textbook in his own classes at The Lewisburg Seminary. Sommerville was influenced by Dewey's writings on progressive education, particularly where he emphasized abandoning rote memorization in favor of a learning-by-doing approach. Dewey wrote extensively about the role of education in a democracy. He further believed that psychology was a tool for achieving philosophical goals, such as finding the principles to achieve a just and fair society. The themes were already ingrained in Sommerville, and as noted earlier, he was already a disciple, especially on the role of education within a democracy.

Robert Woodworth and Edward Thorndike were two of the major researchers who investigated and played a role in laying to rest the "doctrine of formal disciplines." This doctrine, with its emphasis on exercising the faculties of the mind so as to make it more agile for higher thought processes, was definitely subject oriented. While Dewey was forcefully calling for better teacher training and for schools to become more student-oriented rather than topic-oriented, Woodworth and Thorndike published their results. Essentially, they found that only elements which are common or similar between tasks will be facilitated by the mastery of one before the other, that learning one task can in fact interfere with another task if they are opposing in some way. Their research on the transfer of training significantly added to the study of *learning as a process* rather than assuming that certain learning was necessary simply to exercise the mind.[7]

Richard Sommerville was not only influenced by Thorndike and Dewey, but philosophically, he also was compatible with Robert Woodworth. Neither was doctrinaire. Both took an eclectic approach in psychology and accepted any empirically based research technique that would best address the question. They placed emphasis on the individual and how he or she processed information, and both thought that all human behavior was adaptive. That is to say, they both emphasized that individuals act in direct response to environmental factors but are not limited by them. Woodworth popularized the idea of human "drives" to describe motivation, which was his special interest, but Sommerville questioned this as a full explanation of human motivation.[8]

Sommerville's doctoral studies were undertaken at a time when the area of psychometrics had already been established in the discipline of psychology. Robert Woodworth was a doctoral student of James Cattell who developed the program at Columbia, and who was one of the first psychometricians in the United States. Although Cattell was fired from Columbia in 1917 for his outspoken pacifism,[9] during his years there he was, along with Clark Wissler, his graduate student and later curator of the Department of Anthropology of the American Museum of Natural History in New York, the first to "apply the processes of mathematical correlation to the problem of psycho-physical relationships."[10] Sommerville's dissertation was in many ways a continuation of their earlier work.

During the fifty years prior to Sommerville's doctoral studies, one of the most popular research areas was the relationship between mental abilities and physical and sensory characteristics. Essentially, the question was whether or not one could accurately predict intellectual abilities from various physical traits. The long-standing notion that a sane mind resided only in a healthy body had led many researchers from different disciplines to look for relationships between physical traits and mental ability. The idea that quick implies smart persists even to this day.

When simple correlations, such as height and

weight, did not show relationships with intellect (except in some cases where the work was done using techniques that were sometimes unscientific or where atypical population pools were studied, such as institutionalized mentally handicapped subjects), more complex bodily measures were combined to form indices and then correlated. Sometimes the lack of correlation was credited to imprecise measurement, to the lack of adequate statistical techniques, or to the need for a proper index.

Sometimes the research was not done strictly within the guidelines of good science and was done for perhaps social reasons rather than scientific. For example, in 1869, Francis Galton published a series of studies on *Hereditary Genius* in which he concluded that famous men and their family ancestors (men of accomplishment who were assumed to be highly intelligent), tended to be above average in height and weight. That these people also occupied positions of wealth and, therefore, had better diets which do correlate with height and weight, and that they had access to a better education as compared to the general population, were not seen as compounding factors.

Richard Sommerville credited A.T. Poffenbarger, a professor at Teachers' College, with suggesting that he look at complex sensory and motor correlates of success. Success, as defined in Sommerville's dissertation, was not solely based on grades or I.Q. tests, but on participation in extracurricular activities and academic honors. These activities included memberships in social, literary, and academic organizations, such as the campus Greek societies, sports activities, and part-time work activities, as well as the commute distance to the school. Also, academic honors, such as being on the Dean's List and election to *Phi Beta Kappa*, were factored in. The index was arranged such that the greater the number of physical activities and the higher the scholastic attainment, the higher the index.

Points were deducted if the student had ever received a letter of warning from the dean or had been placed on probation. He assumed that the student was in school expecting to get an education, so therefore, grades were counted as double over the extracurricular activities.[11]

Clark Wissler had suggested that he compare his derived Success Index with some of the body build indices that had been developed by Dr. Charles Davenport who was attempting to develop a screening device for the selection of conscripts in the military services. Wissler also suggested that he include some facial measures that may indicate some glandular disturbances. This latter research was then underway at the Presbyterian Hospital in New York City. Sommerville accepted Wissler's recommendations and set out to replicate some of Cattell's measurements using more refined criteria and newer statistical techniques, known as partial correlations. He focused on physical, sensory, and psychological correlates of success among undergraduate students at Columbia University.

The anthropometric measures included height; sitting height; weight; head length, width and height; leg and arm length; face length and width; chest circumference; nose length and width; interpupillary space, width and length of the eye opening; infradental-menton, or the height of the lower face; the horizontal ramus, or length of the horizontal part of the jaw; the gonial angle, or angle between the cheek and jaw; and the subcostal angle, or angle between the ribs. As measures of physical and motor capacity, he included vital breath capacity; strength of grip; steadiness tests; tapping responses; aiming; and jumping. Tests of sensory capacity included auditory and visual acuity; discrimination of weights; and discrimination of lines. For tests of attention and perception he collected data to measure the retention of an array of objects presented visually; letter cancellations from Spanish prose (accuracy against speed was measured); and geometric form naming.[12]

Sommerville's work was one of the first, if not the first, to develop a Success Index by which factors other than intelligence tests, such as grades and performance in outside activities, like athletics and journalism, as well as social activities could be included. These activities were included because it was felt that only the healthiest and the brightest could have high grades and also be highly involved in extracurricular activities. If there was anything to the long held notion that physical and sensory functioning could be used to predict mental functioning, then the Success Index should show it, or so he argued.

Sommerville presented his work with attention to minute details of measurement and mathematical calculations. He ran correlations between each factor of his Success Index and all the sensory, physical, and motor skills which he had meticulously defined. Then he combined scores to form weighted indexes and cross-compared the physical traits. No correlations were found which could even remotely suggest that any of the physical, sensory, or motor responses could predict success. (Richard once said that he collected all that data and he "got ZIP"!) The only interesting data included actual documentation that over the years the college students were becoming taller, more robust, and physically fit. He reported that this finding held true not only at Columbia, but also at other schools where such research had taken place as well. Sommerville credited better diet, an emphasis on physical fitness, and better living conditions as responsible for the increases in physical growth among college students.

An ambitious project with its minute and detailed physical measurements, as prescribed by the anthropologists, and the excruciating statistical analyses (before calculators), could only be undertaken by someone of Sommerville's energy level and interest in statistics. He studied 117 students, taking thirty-four different measurements in March and April of 1924. One hour per subject was required to complete the battery of tests, and the detailed comparisons and cross-comparisons had to have consumed all of his time throughout the remaining spring and summer months. The degree was completed in December of 1924 and formally awarded in June of 1925.[13]

Sommerville's efforts in this compilation of detailed data did not go unrewarded or unnoticed. Not only was he awarded the doctorate, but also his work was deemed important enough to be published in its entirety in the *Archives of Psychology*, No.75 (1924). Actually, Woodworth started this journal as a forum for publication by the successful doctoral candidates in psychology. The rule for dissertation research was that seventy-five copies had to be bound and left with the library. By forming this journal, obviously this rule could be met, and at the same time, a forum was created for the students' work. Each volume featured a single original research project.

Sommerville's work supplied important data in textbooks written by A.T. Poffenbarger, who was interested in industrial applications of psychometrics. In his 1928 text, *Applied Psychology*, he referenced Sommerville's dissertation as follows:

> The most recent investigations into the functions of the internal secretary organs and their relations to physical development on the one hand, and the development of mentality on the other hand, might seem to suggest the practical utility of such indicators. These findings have great scientific interest but there is scarcely any hope of their practical application. Where the relationship between structure and conduct has not been actually zero, it has been so slightly positive as to make

prediction for vocational purpose quite impossible. For a survey of literature and original data on this question, see R.C. Sommerville.... [14]

Donald G. Patterson of the University of Minnesota wrote a book titled, *Physique and Intellect*, published in 1930, which presented an historical overview of laymen's and even accredited scientists' determinations that somehow man's physical body and intelligence are related. He carefully reviewed the accumulated research literature on the subject and demonstrated quite clearly that no relationships had been found. In so doing, he cited Sommerville's work rather extensively. Sommerville's finding paralleling height and weight with performance on the Thorndike Intelligence Test was used to question the classic Galtonian view that men of genius tend to be above average in both. His measurement of head length, width, and height was reported to have "definitely disproved" assertions by S.D. Porteus, a specialist in mental retardation, that intellect could be predicted by the product of these three measures. His measures of head shape, otherwise known as the cephalic index, scotched notions that head shape could be used to predict intellect. Finally, under the subtitle, "Additional evidence on Body Build and Intelligence,"[15] Patterson reported Sommerville's indices on body build to show that mental status could not be predicted by either a single or combined measures of physical traits.[16]

Other authors of general textbooks cited particular sections from his larger work. His finding comparing cumulative grade point averages and performance on an intelligence test, where he had found a correlation of r = .40, was featured in a 1947 text by Robert S. Woodworth and B.G. Marquis titled, *Psychology*, to illustrate that while intelligence is a factor in determining college grades, other factors must be operating as well.[17] Similarly, his work was cited in Kimball Young's 1947 text titled, *Personality and Problems of Adjustment*.[18]

Other researchers cited his general findings, specific results, or statistical techniques in their journal articles. Edwin G. Flemming used Sommerville's techniques for defining a Success Index in his studies concerning the predictive value of certain tests measuring emotional stability in college freshmen.[19] Subsets of Sommerville's findings were discussed by Vernon W. Lemmon in his study of reaction time and its relation to memory, learning, and intelligence.[20] Likewise, his findings were discussed by Young, Drought, and Bergstresser in their studies of social and emotional adjustment of students at the University of Wisconsin.[21]

One reference to Sommerville's work was found in Leigh Van Valen's paper suggesting that certain correlations between brain size and intellect are strong enough to warrant further unbiased study. He did not claim to provide evidence, only to raise the issue. Essentially, Valen reviewed the literature and included references to Sommerville's work as among the better studies done on the issue, but he wrote that "crude measures of intelligence" were used in most all cases in all of the studies. He suggested that a correlation of $r = 0.1$ between external linear measures of cranial size and intelligence is significant enough to be pursued.[22] Apparently, the idea of using physical characteristics to predict intelligence is still alive in some quarters.

The above citations should not be considered as an exhaustive report of the literature for the years prior to 1955. Sommerville's former colleagues and students have referred to him as having had a national reputation. Since he only published one study in the field, it was necessary to see if that work was considered important enough in his day to be cited. In his case, one study was apparently enough.[23] A more important point is that some of the textbooks cited above were used as texts in the psychology courses during the thirties and the forties, thus allowing students to see his work being referenced.

It should be stressed that Sommerville's dissertation was not about intelligence testing or intelligence, but was more in line with combining physical anthropology and psychology. His interests lay in looking at the possibilities that physical characteristics might correlate with success in school and work, an open question at the time. Sommerville was studying at Columbia during a time of highly heated debates on the issue of nature versus nurture and their role on human development. Some of the key players in these debates were at Columbia and/or nearby in various social and political institutions. Psychology generally had come to public attention with the development of intelligence tests and other types of tests particularly for use in recruiting and screening conscripts during World War I. These tests were to become tools utilized by both sides in support of extreme positions on one side or the other. All seemed to agree that psychological testing could be used to study individual differences, but whether these individual differences were endowed by nature or were nurtured was not an issue on which they could agree.

Within psychology, Robert Woodworth, although accused of sitting on the fence, mostly favored the stronger influence of nurture and personal adaptation. Dewey called himself a democratic evolutionist. He agreed with Darwin's theories on the struggle for survival but thought that cultures, governments, and educational opportunities differentiated populations. He argued strongly for equal educational opportunities and democracy. Thorndike, on the other hand, was a convinced hereditarian. He was personally convinced that eugenics was the only hope for improving the human population, and so he was active in the eugenics movement of the nineteen-twenties and early nineteen-thirties. He argued strongly against educational egalitarianism.[24]

Within the field of genetics, Charles Davenport, whom Sommerville consulted about some of the physical measurements for his dissertation, was most actively head of the eugenics movement in the twenties, head of the Galton Society of New York, and director of the Eugenics Record Office at Cold Spring Harbor in New York, among other directorships. On the other hand, within anthropology, Franz Boaz, the famed cultural anthropologist, who was also consulted for the dissertation, was a strong environmentalist and stressed the role of culture on the developing individual.[25]

Where Sommerville stood on the issue can only be surmised. He never missed an opportunity to stress individual freedom of choice, and at one point, he wrote that the personality develops out of native capacities by social contacts and is molded "partly by the environment, partly by the individual's own actions," and that a truly determined individual can rise above his environment.[26] Sommerville probably favored the issue raised by the more important question that arose out of the debates of the twenties. That question was not whether heredity or environmental factors have the greater influence on the developing person, but how these two influences interact on human development.

Sommerville Grows Restless Again

During the 1924-25 academic term, while Sommerville was completing his dissertation, he was also the professor of psychology and dean of the Department of Education at Louisiana Polytechnic Institute, Ruston, Louisiana.[27] He held this position for only one year. The following year, he joined the faculty at Southwestern College at Memphis where he was first appointed the professor of philosophy and then professor of philosophy and aesthetics.[28]

　　While living in Tennessee, he was a member of the Tennessee Academy of Science. During the summers of 1926 and 1927, he taught courses at University of the South.[29] At some point in the spring or summer of 1928, he met Dean Lowell McPherson of Lynchburg College. McPherson had received a master's degree from Columbia in 1925, the same year that Sommerville received his doctorate. Whether they knew each other as students is not known, but McPherson did hire a number of Columbia University graduates during his tenure as dean of Lynchburg College.

　　Richard Sommerville had a tendency to grow restless after successfully working for a number of years in one place. He seemed unable to settle after his resignation at Arkansas College. Apparently, nothing within the three schools in which he was employed could sustain him. Although he once said that he wanted to get back to Virginia, perhaps at this stage of his life, he was looking for an opportunity to assume a role as a philosopher-psychologist.

Notes

　　1. Robert I. Watson, *The Great Psychologists*, 4th edition (Philadelphia: J.B. Lippincott Company, 1978), 368-369.

　　2. Paul R. Palmer, Letter to author with enclosures from the *University Bulletin*, 10 July 1986.

3. Ruby Hemphill, Supervisor of Transcripts and inquiries, Columbia University, Letter to author, 14 November 1983; 31 July 1985.

4. Frederick C. Thorne, "Reflections on the Golden Age of Columbia Psychology," *Journal of the History of the Behavioral Sciences*, (*12*: 159-165, 1976): 160.

5. Melvin H. Marx and William A. Hillix, *Systems and Theories of Psychology*, 3rd edition, (New York: McCraw Hill Book Company, 1979), 95-122.

6. Paul R. Palmer, Curator, Low Memorial Library, Columbia University, Letter to Carol Pollack, 30 June 1986.

7. Robert S. Woodworth and Edward Thorndike, "The Influence of Improvement on One Mental Function Upon the Efficiency of Other Functions," *Psychological Review*, (*8*: 247-261, 1901).

8. For a biographical account of Robert Sessions Woodworth, see David Hothersall, *History of Psychology*, (New York: Random House, 1984), 276, 282ff.

9. Marx and Hillix, *Systems and Theories of Psychology*, 105.

10. Richard Clarke Sommerville, "Physical, Motor, and Sensory Traits," *Archives of Psychology, (75:* 28, 1924), 28.

11. Ibid., 28.

12. Ibid., 55-58.

13. Ruby Hemphill, (1985).

14. A.T. Poffenbarger, *Applied Psychology, Its Principles and Methods*, (New York: D. Appleton and Company, 1928), 260-261.

15. Donald G. Patterson, *Physique and Intellect*, (New York: The Century Company, 1930), 168-169.

16. Ibid., 70, 113-115, 121-123.

17. Robert S. Woodworth and B. G. Marquis, *Psychology*, 4th edition (New York: Henry Holt Company, 1947), 78-81.

18. Kimball Young, *Personality and Problems of Adjustment*, (New York: F.S. Croft and Company, 1947), 316.

19. E.G. Flemming, "The Predictive Value of Certain Tests of Emotional Stability as Applied to College Freshmen," *Archives of Psychology, 96,* (May, 1928).

20. V.G. Lemmon, "The Relation of Reaction Time to Measures of Intelligence, Memory, and Learning," *Archives of Psychology, 94,* (November, 1927).

21. Kimball Young, N.E. Drought, and J. Bergstresser, *Personality and Problems of Adjustment,* (New York: F.S. Croft and Company, 1937), 166-177.

22. Leigh Van Valen, "Brain Size and Intelligence," *The American Journal of Physical Anthropology* (40: 1974): 417-424.

23. Finding these sources meant spending hours in the stacks of Lynchburg College Library, reading old books on the subject. Often Sommerville's handwriting was found in the books, and he often made notations using the Greek alphabet. Because the collection is limited, undoubtedly, many other references to his work could exist. The goal was not to be exhaustive, but to see if students had the opportunity to see his work referenced.

24. David Hothersall, (1984), 276.

25. Ernest Hilgard, *Psychology in America, A Historical Survey,* (San Diego: Harcourt Brace Jovanovich Publishers, 1987), 470-471.

26. Richard Clarke Sommerville, "As a Man Thinketh," *The Prism,* 2 (February, 1940): 16.

27. Richard Clarke Sommerville, (1924), inside cover.

28. Goodbar Morgan, Archivist, Southwestern College, Letter to author with enclosures, 3 June 1983.

29. Richard Clarke Sommerville, *American Men of Science,* 8th edition, Jacques Cattell, Ed., (Lancaster, Pennsylvania: The Science Press, 1947), 2340.

5

A Return to Virginia

Lynchburg College Becomes Home

Richard Sommerville, then fifty-two years old, arrived on the Lynchburg College campus in 1928, yet this traveled man with a preference for small towns may not have intended to make Lynchburg, Virginia, his final home. He once told friends that he chose Lynchburg because he wanted to return to Virginia and that he had interviewed with Dean Lowell McPherson and that they had "hit it off."[1] He had received an offer of a position in psychology from the College of William and Mary the day after he had posted his letter of acceptance to Lynchburg College, but because he had already given his word, he rejected the William and Mary offer.[2]

Over the next twenty years, Sommerville established himself and became a respected professor and member of the Lynchburg community. This setting provided him the opportunity to teach in the three disciplines that he knew most—psychology, education, and philosophy. The local long-standing organizations devoted to the arts provided a forum for him to display and further develop his many talents, particularly in dramatics and painting. Sommerville involved himself with zeal, and because of his personality and character, he attracted attention, even a following who would remember him and see that others would know of him, even after his death. He was to be remembered as "a wise counsel to others," "a friend of the student," and "a man of many parts." A former dean of Lynchburg College and later president of Texas Christian University, Dr. M.E. Sadler, would one day state that Richard Sommerville was "the most fully, beautifully educated man [he] ever knew."[3]

Lynchburg College was established in 1903 as Virginia Christian College, a coeducational institution that had no formal church affiliation or planning. However, because many of the community leaders who invited Josephus Hopwood, the college founder, to start a Christian college in Lynchburg, were associated with the Disciples of Christ (Christian) Church, and over the years they had sought moral and financial support from the church, the Disciples affiliation evolved. Today, it is the second largest institution in covenant with the denomination. In 1919, following two years of careful study by ministers of the church and local citizens, the name of the school was changed to Lynchburg College. During that year, the college began a long-term plan to obtain regional accreditation from the Southern Association of Colleges and Secondary Schools, granted in 1927.[4] With accreditation, this small, church-related, liberal arts college was enjoying a sense of accomplishment and had plans for expanded programs and additional faculty.

Arriving on the campus, Sommerville found a liberal arts school which was similar in many respects to his *Alma Mater*, Hampden-Sydney. However, important differences distinguished the two institutions. Lynchburg College was not only coeducational, but also practical. From its beginning in 1903, applied studies and career training were incorporated within the liberal arts context. On the other hand, student life at Lynchburg College was similar to that of Sommerville's college days. Literary societies, two each for the men and the women, fine arts clubs, language societies, student publications, and a science club all encouraged students to broaden their education. Student life, as it had for the men of Hampden-Sydney, revolved around these organizations. The literary societies were highly visible on the campus and served as a means for socializing as well as a means for practicing literary skills. Over the years, Sommerville, as did many faculty in those days, held membership in some of these student activities, sponsored clubs, gave invited talks, and participated in student plays and recitals. This custom allowed faculty and students to work as well as study together.

A Program Envisioned

Lynchburg's attraction to Sommerville is only one side of the match which was made when Dean McPherson hired him to head the Department of Psychology and Education. The events which followed quickly within his first two years suggest strongly that Sommerville's task was to revamp the psychology-education major and the teacher training program. These two programs were among the largest on the campus in terms of student interests. The college not only had an opening for the chairmanship, but also a need to reorganize the program. During the twenties, following national trends, the school had begun to offer concentrations in major fields. The existing major combining psychology and education was without structure and had mixed goals. While some courses were designed for teaching in the public schools, others were for training Sunday school teachers, without any apparent sequencing. Sommerville's long experience in developing educational programs at the primary, secondary, and college level, and his knowledge and interests in educational philosophy qualified him for the job.

The school's catalogues from 1928-1931 indicate that Sommerville, influenced by his studies at Columbia University, moved quickly to change the emphasis of psychology as a sub-field of teacher training and to establish it as a more defined discipline with an emphasis on experimentation and statistical analysis. Prior to his arrival, students interested in becoming teachers had to major in the subject area in which they planned to teach, and then enroll in education courses designed for teacher preparation. Those who wanted to teach in the elementary grades tended to concentrate on psychology-education so that psychology was mainly a service course for teacher training. To the curriculum in psychology and education Sommerville added courses in Statistics and Tests and Measurements. The former was by then an essential tool of experimental psychology, and the latter was his particular area of expertise. Psychological testing in the form of intelligence and achievement tests was now an important part of the field. As well, growing interest in public education made Tests and Measurements an important part of teacher training. A new introductory sequence was added to replace the existing course in General Psychology which was vaguely described as a "brief consideration of mental phenomena...."[5] The outlined topics for the new course were broader in scope than the original course and were more slanted in the direction of the biological and the behavioral. The second semester sequel stated clearly that some "experimental work" would be required.[6]

The "experimental work" referred to in the course description probably meant data gathering by the student, as well as participation in research as a part of classroom assignments. Indicative of his belief that psychology should be seen as a science, Sommerville sought membership in the college's science club, SPECS, and was accepted on October 1, 1928. Over the years he maintained his membership in this club, giving short papers on topics of interest to the members. Sommerville also used this club as a forum to present research done by himself and by his students. Aside from teaching his views of the discipline, the research assignments involved the students in classroom learning. Under Sommerville, education could not be a passive activity. His approach definitely required active participation by the student, a learning-by-doing approach advocated by John Dewey. His tendency to include data gathering within the classroom assignments was not limited to psychology; such assignments were also part of his courses in philosophy. Some examples of his early presentations included a paper on the topic of multiple personality given before the SPECS Club in 1929, and a research paper on male/female differences in performance on a general abilities test. This later paper was based on research that he collected at Lynchburg College during his first year.[7]

He also revamped the education program, which reflected a strong Dewey influence, to include more study in the philosophy of education. He changed a two-semester sequence in Secondary Education from an emphasis on teacher training and issues of student management to the more social concerns reflective of Dewey's teachings. Principles of Education was added to the curriculum. Here the Dewey influence could not be more apparent even in the cryptic description: "A study of the nature and purpose of education; original nature of man; modification through learning; education as a social function; control of education in a democracy."[8]

Dewey was not the only person from Columbia University who influenced Sommerville. A. I. Gates, Thorndike's colleague and successor at Teachers College, wrote two popular introductory texts for educational psychology which Sommerville used. The first, *Psychology for Students of Education* (1923), was designed by Gates to be a first course in psychology for teachers. The other, *Elementary Psychology* (1929), was designed by Gates to be a first course for psychology majors. In addition to texts by Arthur Gates, Sommerville also used books by Robert Woodworth. Thus for the first several years, Sommerville taught essentially two different introductory psychology courses every semester. Moreover, Sommerville incorporated a "Techniques of Study" course in the curriculum. Here the students were instructed on how to take lecture notes, improve listening skills, and organize notes so that they could become "more efficient" learners. This course was required of all freshmen unless a special exemption was given. Although this course was not new to the curriculum, Sommerville was responsible for developing and teaching it throughout his years at Lynchburg College. The practice of including study habits training within the curriculum illustrated the varied applications of educational psychology. Just as the discipline was addressing issues of good teaching, it was also concerned with developing ways to teach students how to learn.

During his second year, Sommerville received an additional appointment as the professor of philosophy while remaining as head of the Department of Psychology and Education. Prior to Sommerville's arrival, courses in philosophy were available on alternate year offerings, and were taught by Dr. Stuart Grainger, who also taught all courses in economics, social studies, and political science.

Although part-time faculty and other full-time faculty from other disciplines were teaching within the education curriculum, Sommerville's new position essentially gave him administrative control over all three subject areas.

Although he changed the offerings in philosophy to reflect his special interests and expertise, he maintained the stated purpose of the place of philosophy in the curriculum as it had appeared in previous catalogues and made it the rationale for a new joint-major in philosophy and psychology. According to the catalogue:

> A major may be taken in Philosophy and Psychology, jointly. The object in offering these courses is to give the college student, first, an understanding of and practice in using the laws of thought that may be competent to judge when he has accurate information; second, theory and practice in the formation of moral judgments that he may be able to will the right; third, a view of life as a whole that he may be able to escape a one-sided outlook and may have some appreciation of the dignity, significance and value of the human personality.[9]

Sommerville maintained the standard twenty-four hour requirement. Six hours of General Psychology, Logic, and Problems of Philosophy were required with the remaining four courses selected from Statistics, Social Psychology, Tests and Measurements, Adolescent Psychology, Aesthetics, and Ethics.

From the beginning, as had been the rule at Hampden-Sydney, Sommerville limited enrollments in all philosophy courses to students with junior and senior status, a policy that lasted until the end of his teaching career. When he arrived on the campus, a course in philosophy was not required for graduation. In the mid-thirties, when a course in philosophy was added as a general education requirement, it was open only to juniors and seniors. He believed that philosophy was not a subject for which freshmen were ready. He saw philosophy as the discipline that served to integrate all other disciplines so other more factually based course work should be taken in the first two years of general studies.

Like Dewey, Sommerville saw psychology as the introduction to philosophy. The purpose of all study was to strive and to understand social problems, to gain personal understanding, and to cope with a diverse, complex, and ever changing society. He described Logic as "the study of the principles governing valid reasoning processes."[10] The course in Problems of Philosophy was described, in part, as the study of "the outstanding problems which have held the attention of thoughtful men from the beginning of reflective thinking in Greece to the present day."[11] The study of Ethics was "the search for a rational basis for the moral law," and he wrote that there would be "practical applications of the law to problems of the present day."[12] And finally, the course in Aesthetics, the highest num-bered course, was described as an "examination into the qualities causing excellence in the higher arts (architec-ture, music, poetry, painting and sculpture)." The purpose of the course was to help the student "to perceive beauty wherever it appears and to appreciate it more highly."[13]

Sommerville departed sharply from tradition, how-ever, in that he dictated not only the major requirements, which was within his purview, but also precisely specified the general education requirements for his majors! Col-lege policy allowed major programs some latitude in specifying general education requirements within a given set of courses. However, Sommerville not only specified more courses than anyone else, but also went outside the guidelines. From his program, one is able to see that Sommerville was following the policies like those at Hampden-Sydney a quarter of a century earlier when the curriculum was set for the student by the faculty and electives were only allowed within specified guidelines.

In Sommerville's program at Lynchburg College (aside from the usual requirements in Bible, English grammar and literature, personal hygiene, and physical education) the student was required to take twelve hours of French or German. No other major except biology and chemistry specified these two languages, as the preferred language of the day was still Latin. However, French and German had become the preferred languages of the sciences, and Sommerville was fluent in French and highly literate in German. Other requirements included twelve hours of history (as opposed to the usual six) which had to include Greek and Roman History as well as two semesters of History of the Middle Ages. All students were required to complete eight hours of biology and an additional eight hours of another laboratory science which could be either chemistry, physics, or Comparative Vertebrate Anatomy and Comparative Vertebrate Embryology. Finally, instead of the usual three hours, the student had to take fourteen hours of sociology, Introduction to Social Science (a two-hour requirement for all freshmen), Sociology, Foundation Course (a six-hour sophomore-level sequence for majors), and Social Problems (a senior-level six-hour sequence).[14]

The more intensive study of history, the social sciences, and the natural or biological sciences required of the philosophy-psychology major not only mirrored Sommerville's interests, but also reflected his views of what an educated person should know. Over the years, Sommerville gained the reputation for being very knowledgeable in the sciences of his day, for being able to discuss current social issues with authority, and for knowing political history as well as philosophical arguments. While his courses in psychology were to undergo many different descriptions over the years of his tenure, the descriptions of his four courses in philosophy remained the same. His students were to remember him for his teaching of these courses more than any others to the extent that more than one former colleague and student wondered why he studied for his doctorate in psychology and not in philosophy. The answer is very simple. Richard Sommerville never simply worked toward a degree, he studied areas in which he had interest. He pursued the new science of psychology because he was interested in what information it had to offer, not as an end, but as means of understanding human nature. From psychology Sommerville also sought the tools he could use in helping students learn. Since he believed that philosophy was the discipline which integrated all other disciplines including psychology, sociology, history, religion, the arts and all other sciences, he so organized his new joint-major to reflect this view.

The Program is Lost

This joint-major in this particular form was short-lived. It lasted only three years. Only one student is listed as ever having completed this program before it fell victim to the exigencies caused by the Great Depression. From 1930 through two-thirds of the decade, the depression threatened the school repeatedly. It took its toll on the academic programs, causing much instability, as various ideas were tried.

Early in the decade, a consultant was called in to suggest ways to reorganize the academic programs, because the school had learned they did not meet the financial requirements of the Southern Association. A team arrived to study the academic programs. Among the many recommendations, two affected Sommerville

directly: 1) to move philosophy into a division with religion, and 2) to readjust the course offerings in education
and psychology so that two faculty members could handle
all course work.[15]

These recommendations led to the immediate elimi-
nation of the joint-major in psychology and philosophy.
The Techniques of Study course was dropped, and many
of the remaining courses in psychology, philosophy and
education were offered on alternate years. Sommerville
continued to teach all of the courses within philosophy and
psychology and he returned to teaching some of the education courses that he had two years earlier.

From 1932 to 1936, the courses, particularly in
psychology, were somewhat in flux, as the college experi-
mented with the quarter system for three years (1934-
1937). Statistics was dropped after 1934 and Tests and
Measurements was eliminated after 1935. Neither course
was to be taught by him again, although they were his
specific areas of expertise. After 1935, the only remaining
courses in psychology were the two-semester sequence in
General Psychology, Educational Psychology, Social
Psychology, and the newly renamed Mental Adjustment,
which was nothing more than a title change for the existing
course in Abnormal Psychology. He continued to teach
Problems in Philosophy, Aesthetics, Logic, Ethics, and
Principles of Education. The education courses had to
remain somewhat intact throughout these years because
they were required by the State Board of Education for
teacher certification.

Educational Goals Salvaged

While the program that he had envisioned was
eliminated, he remained undaunted. In 1939-40 the joint-

major appeared again on the books, even though only five courses were available in philosophy and the number of psychology offerings had been drastically reduced in scope and in number. Moreover, the course descriptions for the psychology offerings now carried a personal development theme. The course in General Psychology read:

> An introductory course in which especial emphasis is laid upon the application of psychological principles to the actual problems met by living students, in the hope of helping these young people to a more adequate adjustment to life.[16]

Likewise, upper-level courses carried the personal development theme. Although the course descriptions moved away from the statistical-experimental and biological orientation, Sommerville did not change his mind about these approaches. He still assigned students to collect data as a part of classroom assignments. Although he allowed his membership in SPECS to lapse during 1933-35, he returned to active participation from 1936 onward. Some of his presentations include a paper on the characteristics of brain waves,[17] and "The Nazi Attitude Toward Science" in which he stated the concern that, "The Germans believe that science is national and racial, and therefore, German Science is unlike science as learned in other parts of the world."[18] Another paper, "Our Aging Population," looked at the 1940 census and discussed what would happen if the then current downward trend in child birth in light of the increased life expectancy continued. Indicating that "we are rapidly becoming a nation of elders," he predicted that by 1980, persons sixty-five and older would account for 14.4% of the population and that two-fifths of the total population would be over forty-five. While he indicated that the predicted changes in the population would lead to social and political problems, he said that his purpose was first to present the facts and that the listener should "let your mind begin to dwell upon them."[19]

Most of his presentations involved basic research conducted by him and his students enrolled in both the philosophy and psychology classes. Included were topics in ESP;[20] stereotyping, in which occupations were assigned to photographs of persons;[21] emotions as experienced by students in a 24-hour period, with attention given to the time of day in which those emotions were more apt to occur;[22] handedness, or preferences in the use of the left and right hand on selected tasks;[23] and an experiment in aesthetics where students were asked to measure rectangles that they found pleasing, the results were analyzed with implications for marketing and manufacturing strategies.[24] Finally in 1947, he presented the results of a three year investigation on students' preferences for personality characteristics which were seen as pleasing or displeasing.[25]

His beliefs about the place of philosophy never changed but intensified in relation to his goals. The Division of Religion and Philosophy by now included courses in the fine arts. Among the stated purposes of this division were two goals for which Sommerville is most remembered. His original goal, "To comprehend broadly the philosophy interests of mankind" now included the phrase "and [to] form a personal philosophy of life." His second goal was "to respond appreciatively and actively to beauty in music and art."[26] The first goal translated into a direct assignment. This assignment was that any student enrolled in his first course in philosophy had to write a required paper on his or her personal philosophy of life. Mr. William Shackelford, his former student, has been able to establish that at least by 1934, any student who enrolled in Philosophy 301 did so knowing that this was a requirement. Before the curriculum reforms in the mid-thirties, no course in philosophy was required for a general education. Therefore, students elected to enroll in a philosophy course, unless they were enrolled in majors where it was required. Following the reforms, six hours of philosophy were required as a part of general education. Thereafter, all students who received a degree from Lynchburg College had to study under Dr. Sommerville and had to face this task.

He is well remembered for his emphasis on the personal philosophy of life. If the students took it seriously, it was considered a learning experience. For others it was seen as a challenge that they did not welcome, for if they did not comply with his instructions as to what a personal philosophy should include, or if they simply wrote their likes and dislikes, he gave low marks. This assignment was no idle whim on Sommerville's part but rather indicative of his philosophy of education. Just as the students of psychology and aesthetics should conduct research not only as an intellectual exercise but also to learn about themselves as mini-scientists, so the students of philosophy should use their studies to learn where they stand on important matters. What they believed was not as important as how they arrived at their conclusions through reasoning, logic, and experience. For Sommerville, all study should focus on utility to the student if education was to have purpose at all.

Richard Sommerville arrived on the Lynchburg College campus at the age of fifty-two, full of vigor and vitality. Although he obviously had plans for his curriculum and what was needed to educate the students, social and economic forces came into play which could have devastated a much younger man. Had he been twenty-two and without the previous thirty years of surviving disappointments, the story of his life probably would have been different. However, armed with the academic and personal lessons of his past, and bolstered by his sheer intellect and ability to range over the curriculum, Richard Sommerville could always be an effective teacher, no matter his circumstance. Sommerville was schooled in the notion that the professor should be widely read and should command as many disciplines as possible, not as end, but as a means for living. He further felt that an education should provide information for the students so that they could use it to make wise decisions in life, and be happy, useful, and productive citizens. When his program was lost, he was not. He simply taught his vision.

Notes

1. William Shackelford, interview with author, 11 March 1983.

2. Melva Adams, interview with author, 6 June 1983.

3. Meredith Norment, Jr., "An Appreciation," written on the occasion of the announcement of the Sommerville Scholarship Fund, (1964).

4. Orville Wake, "A History of Lynchburg College, 1903-1953," (Unpublished doctoral dissertation, 1957), 181ff.

5. *Catalogue of Lynchburg College,* (1927-28), 62, 79.

6. Ibid., 79.

7. *Minutes, SPECS Club Meetings, 1922-1952*, Lynchburg College Archives.

8. *Catalogue of Lynchburg College, (1927-28)* 62, 79; *The Bulletin of Lynchburg College, 3,* 3, (1928-29), 45, 58, 77.

9. *The Bulletin of Lynchburg College 4*, 1 (1929-30), 73; *The Catalogue of Lynchburg College, (1927-28),* 73.

10. Ibid., 73.

11. Ibid., 74.

12. Ibid.

13. Ibid.

14. Ibid., 42, 80-81.

15. *Minutes of the Executive Committee*, January 30, 1933.

Lynchburg College Archives.
16. *The Catalogue of Lynchburg College, (1939-1940)*, 72.
17. *Proceedings of the SPECS Club*, 1, 1936-37. Lynchburg College Archives.
18. Ibid., April 13, 1942.
19. Ibid., January 11, 1944.
20. *Proceedings of the SPECS Club (2*, 1937-38). Lynchburg College Archives.
21. Ibid., (*3*, 1938-39).
22. *Minutes*, (May 13, 1940).
23. Ibid., (April 8, 1943).
24. Ibid., (May 8, 1945).
25. Ibid., (May 12, 1947).
26. *The Catalogue of Lynchburg College (1937-38)*, 46.
Sommerville met his second goal through his involvement with performing arts programs and by giving lectures on music and art to students during assemblies.

6

"As A Man Thinketh"...

Believing that the teacher should serve as the role model as well as advisor to his students, Dr. Sommerville did more than simply ask the students to write their personal philosophies of life. For him, this task was no ordinary writing assignment but a real task with real merit—the culmination of a semester's work in Problems of Philosophy. In 1940 an overview of his personal philosophy of life was summarized for the *Prism*, the Lynchburg College literary magazine.

As A Man Thinketh
by Richard C. Sommerville

All knowledge, in the final analysis, rests upon belief. The chemist and the physicist believe that they deal with an ordered nature in which the law of cause and effect is operative; the mathematician believes that the laws of number and the axioms of geometry are true and he accepts them without proof. If this be true for the exact sciences, it is, of course, so for other fields of investigation.

111

The beliefs which underlie one's interpretation of experience as a whole constitute one's philosophy. And when one consciously endeavors to attain by reasoning a consistent, coherent set of such beliefs, he is said to philosophize. It is not necessary to prove one's beliefs; the geometrician does not prove his axioms, he accepts them as reasonable. So the requirements for tenable beliefs are: (1) They shall be reasonable, not absurd; (2) They shall not be contradictory to other attested facts; (3) They shall not be mutually inconsistent; (4) They shall be as simple, few and comprehensive as possible; (5) They shall be fruitful in explanation.

It is a profitable experience for one to take time out occasionally in order to examine his world beliefs. This is equivalent to a kind of intellectual inventory. Thereby some outmoded lumber may be discarded, some valuable new ideas added, and the whole may be molded into more harmonious shape. In the end one gains confidence by seeing more clearly where he stands. Especially is this important in the present time of storm and stress, when, the old sailing marks being befogged, we are caught in confusing crosscurrents of events and blown upon by conflicting winds of doctrine.

WHAT I BELIEVE[1]

I believe that whether I look at a simple crystal, a blade of grass, or the vast reaches of the universe as revealed by the stars in their courses, I am experiencing a cosmos that came into being not by blind chance but by a Cosmic Design.

I believe that back of the things as we see them, back of the cosmic design, there is a Cosmic Mind. Our reason demands a first cause, or a creator; my thinking finds it here more readily than elsewhere.

I believe that purpose is at work in the universe and that it can be as effective as cause. Whether an event is interpreted as the result of cause or of purpose depends upon whether one looks backward or forward; many events are capable of both interpretations. Cause is no more tangible than purpose; in either case we actually see only sequence of events. If we do not always discern the purpose of happenings, it may be for the same reason that we do not always know causes — lack of sufficiently comprehensive knowledge.

I believe that cosmic design, cosmic mind and cosmic purpose point to God. I say no more, for to attempt to define Him would be to limit Him.

I believe, as a corollary of the preceding, that religion in the sense of "belief in a power not ourselves that makes for righteousness" and a desire to come into harmonious relationship with it is not an illusion, but a justified activity of the human spirit. Our feeble aspirations for good point, as William James says, to a "Divine More" of the same in the universe.

I believe that when one experiences beauty, whether in a mathematical demonstration, a crystal, a flower, a landscape, a sparkling vault of stars or in a work of human art, one is not far removed from experiencing religion. Both experiences are poignantly joyous, both give us intimations of something high and noble which we only dimly apprehend.

I believe that there is such a thing as absolute truth, though at present much, perhaps most, of the knowledge which we acquire through our imperfect perception and reasoning is partial and relative. Yet I believe that as progress continues men will approximate nearer and nearer to *the* truth. It is possible that some, at least, may be able to reach it now through intuition.

I believe that man is free, but that each individual can increase or diminish his freedom by the use which he makes of deliberative choice. Of course it is obvious that many human acts, such as organic processes, reflexes and well-fixed habits, are quite mechanical; it is in moments of choice that freedom appears. Even here some persons surrender freedom by submitting themselves to the control of impulse, prejudice, or the opinions of the group. But others learn to increase their freedom by lengthening their margin of deliberation.

I believe that personality in the sense of an integrated self developed out of native capacities by social contacts is molded partly by the environment, partly by the individual's own actions, and that a determined individual can increase his own share in shaping his personality. That is, he can rise above his environment. And I believe that disciplined, brave, wise and just personality is one of the noblest and most precious things that we can know.

I believe that such personality, so difficult to create, may well be worth cosmic preservation, in its spiritual aspects. But whether the spirit survive the death of the body or no, I believe death in due time is, like birth, of the order of nature and that whatsoever follows it will be well.

I believe that amid the variations of moral practice to be observed in different peoples and at different levels of culture there is discoverable a central core of moral principle which abides through the changes. That moral law may be stated thus: That act is right which most promotes the perfecting of selves; not myself, but the selves of whom I am one.

I believe that therefore the most enlightened and moral state will exemplify some form of truly representative government, because such a government seems best fitted to promote the development and perfecting of selves. It does not follow that every people should have this form imposed upon them immediately, for some may not yet be qualified for it; but I believe that it is the ideal toward which mankind moves.

I believe in the impartial discussion of debatable propositions. Here the college has a special responsibility, for it seeks to produce as its best achievement; enlightened and independent thinkers. How can this be done without presenting all sides of a question? Hence, if a college opens its rostrum to a speaker who advocates only one point of view, it should presently invite a speaker to present the opposite view. To be specific, after hearing a militarist, I would even like to hear a pacifist, and *vice versa*. In this day of propaganda, one of the best ways to combat it is to encourage young people to preserve open minds until they have examined all arguments.

I believe that modern, large scale industry requires the pooling of endeavor and of financial resources and hence that capitalism is not *per se* an evil, but may be a means of increased good. Without such pooled resources, we could not have automobiles, refrigerators, radios and many other comforts and conveniences; they would cost too much. *Science News Letter* (Dec. 30, 1939) states that "a New Jersey machinist as a hobby built an automobile entirely by hand, and working five hours a day average, he spent twelve years on the job." I figure that, on a conservative estimate, the cost of this machine for labor alone would be $18,000.00. The pooling of labor and capital produces a better one for as many hundred or less. The question then is not, shall we permit capital, but who shall own it, private individuals or the public? I favor a combination of these two, namely private ownership under control by governmental regulation.

I believe that war is a hideous evil.

I believe that some things are more evil than war. For instance, to lose the stamina that makes a free man, to surrender to an aggressor without struggle liberties dearly won by the blood and sacrifice of our forebears, or to be selfishly indifferent to aggression upon other peoples.

I believe that, since the motives of men are rarely simple, but usually complex, it is vain to seek a single cause for war. Hence I believe that those who tell us that all wars are due to population pressure, or to economic rivalry, or to munitions makers, and so on, are guilty of the error of over-simplification. They are prone to start with a theory and then force the facts to support it. My guess is that there are many causes for war and that any particular war arises from a complex of such causes, some of which have their roots far back in time.

I believe that pacifism is not the remedy for war, as the world is today, but may indeed lead to it by inviting aggression. Since Munich I have had a growing opinion that, but for the strong and outspoken trend toward pacifism in the democracies which, by partially disarming them, made Munich unavoidable and which misled Hitler into concluding that they would not fight under any circumstances, the world would not be in the state that it is now. I take a realistic view here; just as there are individuals who are law-abiding only through fear of the police, so there are national governments that will observe the comity of nations only when confronted with force. If they see no force to fear, they will take what they want. Should you then say to them, "Naughty, naughty, (sic) they will push you in the face, take something more and laugh.

I believe that the remedy for war is some form of world government, similar to the League of Nations, but provided with police powers in the shape of an army and navy for enforcing order. Men live in peace in small communities by committing the sword to the arm (police) of government; likewise in the large community of the state; likewise in larger federations of states, as in the United States of America. The method by which peace has been secured in portions of the earth seems to point clearly to the road by which it is to be attained for the whole world. This road may not be traversed to the happy end in my lifetime nor yours, but we can set our faces toward it and our feet upon the beginning of it.

I believe in progress, in an ongoing process that results in the gradual betterment not only of man's material and economic environment, but also of his general intelligence, his moral behavior and his richness and fullness of life. This progress is not along a straight line with a continuous upward slope, but is marked by fluctuations and is subject to regressions; with respect to several aspects of society we seem to be near the trough of a regression at present. But the long view of recorded history will reveal a general upward direction of development.

I believe that progress, by the nature of its course, requires time and patience. For this reason many of us fret about it and despair of it. We are not content to do our bit and then wait in patience for the fruition of our endeavor in the fullness of time. We want what we want when we want it, now, if not sooner. It is corrective of this impatient temper to consider for how brief a time, astronomically speaking, man had been struggling upward and how much time probably lies ahead of him. Using figures taken from Sir James Jeans, I have calculated that, if the age of the earth be represented by one day of 24 hours, or 86,400 seconds, then the existence of man on the earth will fall within the last 13 seconds of that day, and the growth of European civilization from the time of Homer will have occurred within the very last thirteen-hundredths of a second; whereas the predicted future life of the human race on earth will be 500 such days, or 43,200,000 seconds. Such findings from the astronomers may well cause us to marvel that man has accomplished so much in so short a time and encourage us to hope for immensely greater achievements in the future. They should help us to follow Spinoza's advice to look at things under a kind of aspect of eternity, which is good medicine for all sorts of fretting.

I believe that ideals are necessary for progress. People do not readily awake from smug complacency and gird themselves for the hard road upward until they catch the gleam of a vision high and splendid. Ideals are most effective for action when made visible in personalities that we can respect and revere. Hence I believe that heroes also are important for progress. Here I am disposed to point an accusing finger at the literary realists and biographical debunkers who are so zealous in magnifying the brute crudities of life and the frailties of eminent men that they tend to rob human nature of its significance and dignity.

Thereby they do us, especially our young people, a great disservice. For when ideals are shattered and heroes toppled to the mire, what is left in life worth striving for except its animal satisfactions? "Where there is no vision, the people perish." The totalitarian leaders realize this and they have sedulously set before their young people ideals to arouse their enthusiasm, heroes to enlist their following. Thereby they have welded their youth into powerful, consolidated forces for national and world achievement. Compare this result with the confused, demoralized youths of America who have been taught by their reading that ideals are vain and heroes venial.

I believe in the high value of human liberty and am thankful that I live in a country where it is still possible for a man to stand up in public and, with due regard for dissenting opinion and the common good, say what he honestly thinks. Priceless liberty; may we guard it well![2]

....So He Teaches

Sommerville's personal philosophy can be compared with the reading list for his course, Problems of Philosophy. The list of required readings for the course he taught in 1942-43 has been made available by Mrs. Lorraine Flint, his former student. The readings were organized around topics, and although the exact course outline is not available, there were obvious themes, such as duty, obligation, and citizenship. From the readings one can easily detect the influences on Sommerville's personal beliefs. He selected original works by philosophers, psychologists, physical, and biological scientists, and from those who, like William James and William Lowe Bryan, identified themselves as philosopher-psychologists.[3] While Sommerville's psychology was mostly influenced by professors at Columbia University, his philosophy assignments were more influenced by students or members of Harvard's Department of Psychology and Philosophy.

Chief among these were William James and his disciples, such as William E. Hocking, Mary Calkins, Charles Dunbar Broad, and Ralph B. Perry. Also affiliated with Harvard were the British philosopher-mathematician, Alfred North Whitehead, and the psychologist-philosopher, William McDougall, among others.[4]

With its emphasis on the history of philosophy and science and the contributions of these disciplines to the important questions of the day, the course content was very similar to the course in moral philosophy which he took at Hampden-Sydney. Emphasis was placed on the mind and the questions of knowing, thinking, and feeling in an ever-changing universe. However, the greater emphasis concerned the duty of the citizen and the challenges of ethics in a complex, changing society. Many of the reading assignments addressed the place of God and religion in light of the new developments in the sciences and the challenges of the theory of evolution.

Likewise, the structure and reading selections of his course were reflective of his philosophy of education; he believed in free and open inquiry and the balanced presentation of points of view, without dogma. He encouraged open inquiry by assigning readings from authors like James and his disciples who summarized differing philosophies from opposing points of view.

Philosophy Must be Functional

As indicated in previous chapters, Sommerville believed that all education should have utility for the student if it is to have lasting value. He also believed that the student should study from the masters of any discipline to see what they thought and how they arrived at their thinking. A student's goal was not to memorize a series of facts but to use the information for personal growth. Within the course, Richard not only provided a clear demonstration of his view of education, but also bolstered this view with readings by other philosophers. From writings by M.W. Calkins and C.D. Broad, he could emphasize the scope and utility of philosophy as a distinct discipline which must be approached by scientific investigations as opposed to opinions about issues.[5] Accordingly, the student's job is to learn the philosophies of the ages, then to evaluate and criticize them constructively. In this way the student can better develop his or her philosophy of life. In the opening paragraph of his essay, Sommerville echoed Broad's prescription for a philosophy of life. Both agree that personal philosophies should be based on beliefs which are reasonable, not contradictory to known facts, or not mutually inconsistent. They should be simple, few, and as comprehensive as possible. These beliefs become guiding principles against which the student can gage personal behavior and opinions.[6]

For Sommerville, political and social issues should not be unique concerns of any era. Instead, he believed that all social problems evolved over time. For the student, an understanding of this point made political and social issues just as important as the traditional metaphysical issues, perhaps more so. He incorporated these views into his teachings by asking his students to read and study, looking for "integrated wholes," to develop their philosophies for living. He saw the purpose of education as enabling the individual to adjust to his or her social and physical environment. Moreover, the methods of the natural sciences are tools to solve the problems of society. These methods are not final solutions but are instrumentalities for dealing with an always changing and growing human experience.

After considering Richard's educational background, his experience as a teacher, and his philosophy of education, one can see that when the program he had originally set for his students at Lynchburg College was lost, his mission was provide the information more directly within the context of his courses. He wanted to give each student the educational tools to arrive at an integrated understanding of religion, the sciences, philosophy, sociology, history, and the arts. For this reason, only juniors and seniors were allowed to enroll in philosophy courses; students were simply not ready for the task before this time. For him, which particular philosopher the student followed was not important; the process of thinking, integrating, analyzing, and using the information for personal development was the goal.

Human Development is Always Progressing

Sommerville saw human development and human thinking as progressive not regressive. Not only did he specifically address this point in his essay, but also he assigned a selection from Bergson's *Matter and Memory* which argued that the mind and body are united by memory which cannot logically exist in a regression from the present to the past, but it does exist from the past to the present.[7] Both felt that such progress led to the betterment of society, although Sommerville, in the context of World War II, acknowledged that there was a regression in progress! Sommerville's views concerning progress are very understandable. In his lifetime Richard Sommerville had witnessed many inventions that had made life more convenient for people, including the automobile, electricity, the telephone, the radio, oil and gas furnaces, the washing machine, the refrigerator, indoor plumbing, to name but a few. Within factories assembly lines and the development of machinery made factory work much easier and more economical. In spite of the war, Richard maintained a positive outlook.

Above all, Sommerville had a personal faith in human ingenuity, and he was convinced that over the ages human intellect had definitely advanced. In this regard, he was fond of quoting Sir James Jeans' calculations of the age of the earth and extrapolating the data to a twenty-four hour clock to show "that man has accomplished so much in so short a time...." Whenever he wavered in this faith, he would return to history and reflect on the progress that had occurred over the ages, refreshing himself and endeavoring to take the long view of things. He often said that this view could be a cure for all sorts of fretting and could encourage patience, a characteristic that he admired.

Religion and Science do not Conflict

From the course content, his personal statement, and his program goals, Sommerville was indeed a product of the era in the late nineteenth and early twentieth centuries. There were two important developments in the philosophy of the era: the rising prestige of the natural sciences and the belief that reality was dynamic. These two developments came together in the concept of evolution. Thinkers of all disciplines could now recognize that thoughts, ideas, and philosophical theories are outgrowths of culture and change over time. In Sommerville's day it was difficult for religion to be a private matter; one simply had to know where one stood and be willing to take that stand publicly. For Sommerville, religion and science do not conflict. His course list included many original writings by some of the leading scientists and mathematicians of his day, in addition to personal testimonies by philosophers who saw no need for conflict.[8]

During the challenging first three decades of this century, religion and science were thought to be in conflict. While he was living in Arkansas, that state, Tennessee, and Mississippi passed laws forbidding the theories of evolution from being taught in the public schools. Later he was to become a resident of Memphis, Tennessee, while the famous Scopes trial was underway in Dayton. William Jennings Bryan, a conservative Presbyterian Elder who prosecuted Scopes, led in the crusade "against evolution as a destroyer of men's faith" with a large conservative following both within and outside his faith.

Within the Presbyterian denomination, there were many issues subsumed by the debates that split modernism against conservatism. These issues, such as the inerrancy of the Scriptures and the inspiration of the Bible, led to trials of heresy for ministers and laymen alike, including the president of Southwestern College. Before and during the time that Sommerville was teaching philosophy at the Southwestern, rumors about the president's soundness of faith had circulated. Ultimately the president was charged and later cleared of all charges against his orthodoxy in 1930.[9]

Throughout the statement of his personal philosophy and elsewhere, Sommerville wrote about his absolute faith in God, and his students understood that their personal philosophies should address this issue. The readings in his courses supplied many examples of personal testimonies from others. He never shied away from giving his own, leading those who knew him to refer to him always as a "true believer," a "Christian Gentleman." Never to preach fear and damnation nor wage against perceived sin, his personal statements always attested to the advantages of "a belief of something outside ourselves." In 1939 Sommerville wrote:

I now feel that, supported by a large and eminent company, I can without need of apology continue to believe in God, a Spiritual Being in and back of the universe. I can believe that there exists absolute truth, though it be, and probably is, beyond the reach of finite minds. I can refuse to admit that might and convenience make right but rather believe that there exists abiding principles of righteousness and that man's struggle upward towards these shall eventually not be in vain. I can respect my intellectual honesty and decline to say that I admire the coarse and the crude when I believe that man attains to beauty only when he noble spirit within him flowers forth in ordered and harmonious form. I can still hold that the seeker after abiding truth, goodness, and beauty is on the right track when his steps lift him towards the Divine.[10]

Richard Sommerville was a lifelong Presbyterian, and in Lynchburg, so long as his health permitted, he was a regular member of the Westminster Presbyterian Church.[11] Although his obituary in *The Record* of 1963 stated that he was an Elder, according to church records, he had never held a church office. Although friends said that he could have been an Elder, he chose not to. Some say that he did not believe in the practice of "churching" people, and as an Elder he would have to vote on these decisions.

Sommerville agreed with Richard Clarke Cabot that "religion in the 'sense of a belief in a power not ourselves that makes for righteousness' and a desire to come into harmonious relationship with it is not an illusion, but a justified activity of the human spirit." For Richard, religion was very personal and could be experienced anywhere and anytime, but a regular attendance in a house of worship was a time set aside for personal renewal and personal reflection. Selected readings by both Richard Clarke Cabot and William James discussed the role of religion upon reflection, a personal habit that Sommerville encouraged.[12] Interestingly, Cabot, a physician, was a specialist in the treatment of tuberculosis and derived much of his view on human nature from working with his patients. While he was a prolific writer on many topics, this particular set of writings included the value of worship, confession, communion, spiritual fatigue, and recollections, a justification for attendance at a house of worship no matter what one's religious beliefs might be.

Among the assigned readings, perhaps the central article most telling of Sommerville's personal assessment was C. Lloyd Morgan's *Emergent Evolution*. This theory had been around for some time and was popularized by Morgan when, in 1922, he was called to give the Gifford Lectures at the University of St. Andrews in Scotland. His presentations on emergent evolution were published in 1928. The concept of emergent evolution was essentially an argument used by some to show that religion and evolution are not contradictory. The concept of emergent evolution connotes more than the unfolding of events in nature over time; it means that whichever event or element has emerged, it was implicit from the beginning and made explicit through time. Or to use Morgan's words, "In the beginning the end was enfolded."[13]

Morgan argued that a Cosmic Mind was back of this Cosmic Activity and points to God. Emergence started with matter (chemical-physical events), then gave rise to life (physical event), which then gave rise to conscious events (the mind). He assumed that the level of the mind was higher than the level of the body, which was higher than matter. That is, the mind could not exist without life, and life could not exist without a physical basis. Therefore, the universe and all the people in it came into being in accordance with God's plan.

This logic was also used to explain the position of humans in the universe which was obviously elevated because only humans had the powers of the mind. With this elevation came the responsibility for the world that

God had created. For the inhabitants thereof came the duty to responsible citizenship. Morgan's work provides the logical background for Richard Sommerville's views on why the individual must live responsibly, not only within his or her society, but also for all societies because God made humanity responsible for both itself and the world.[14]

A reading by Francis Edward Younghusband stressed that all human beings should have a religious view if religion is to have any service to humanity.[15] This particular selection was a personal testimony in which the author, a professional soldier, stated that science did not destroy his religion, but on the contrary, expanded it. Believing that all men are good, that evil is only superficial, and that the collective whole of mankind is a spiritual thing, Younghusband wrote that people are the spirit which animates the world. Therefore, all people should choose the line of activity for which they are best suited, for all such activity is always part of God's purpose. No calling is menial while another is grand. Therefore, by implication, people should choose to do in life what is best for them and take pride in the doing. As both of these themes were central in Sommerville's thinking and teachings, he believed that each person should work on self-improvement, increase self-awareness, and ultimately, accept one's lot in life. In this regard, he was fond of telling his students to "blow their little tin whistles" or "to beat their little tin drums" in his appeal for them to choose happiness and to be content with who they were. Just as he had lived without apology, never allowing others to tell him what to do, he wanted the same for his students.

Sommerville did not see science as a static amalgamation of facts but an evolving body of information. Readings by Sullivan addressed the point that science was ever changing, and emphasized changes in scientific discoveries after Newton, resulting in science becoming more speculative and allowing more room for individual thought.[16] Further, he saw no reason why a student should not study science. The reading by the agnostic David Hume was added to support the position that every one's nature is to inquire and reason and that all knowledge is a contiguity of ideas.[17] A reading by William James explained that pragmatism was a useful approach for inquiry which, in the view of James, allows for the analysis of all lines of inquiry including metaphysical questions, limiting none, including the search for God.[18] Also included were the readings by Rene Descartes,[19] and "Zeno of Elea."[20] Here, the students read Descartes' well known passage on the act of doubting all but the existence of God. Although the introduction of Zeno's Paradoxes was limited, the use of Dialectics as a tool for use in questioning "truth" was recommended for the student's edification.[21]

Perfection is Known Only Through Intuition

The sixth set of readings presented arguments that perfection can only be intuited and that much must be taken on faith. A passage by Henri Bergson discussed the concept of the perfect absolute which can only be intuited. According to Bergson, although one can only intuit perfection, a point on which Sommerville specifically agreed, *because* one can do this, the individual has an obligation to work on perfecting oneself.[22] Ending this topic was an evaluation by H.W. Carr on Bergson's beliefs that a theory of knowledge and a theory of life are inseparable because knowledge exists for life. Again, the idea that man can only intuit truth and, therefore, all things rest on faith, was emphasized. Clearly, Sommerville's personal statement demonstrates his belief that all truth rests on what one accepts as such. Like Bergson, Sommerville believed that one can only intuit perfection, that it is as ideal which can only be apperceived.

Ethics and Personal Obligations

Sommerville devoted five readings to the topics of ethics, personal responsibility, and doing one's duty by living as a social being.[23] Concern for doing one's duty was not only a recurring theme in the class readings, but also was a personal theme that Sommerville emphasized all his life, beginning with his days at Hampden-Sydney College. A sense of patriotic duty was part of his family heritage.

Sommerville's view of allegiance to high duty meant a willingness to stand up for personal principles of righteousness. One of the principles was the necessity to fight for democracy because "such a government seems best fitted to promote the development and perfecting of selves." In the years leading up to the American involvement in World War II, he was most anxious about the debate over whether or not the United States should become more involved. He did not agree with the noninvolvement policies of the United States or the actions of Neville Chamberlain, the prime minister of England and the French Premier, Edouard Daladier, at the Munich Conference of 1938 where they agreed to give Hitler the Sudetenland. Within the following months, when Hitler took over all of Czechoslovakia, the world may have been stunned, but Sommerville was resolute in his views that there are "worse things than war" and that pacifists were responsible for the rise of Hitler.

In January of 1939 he wrote in mocking tones:

...The great war that seemed improbable has come and gone, leaving wreckage of lives, of wealth and of civilized order in its wake; while another, probably worse, seems even now a-brewing. Tyrants have returned to strut and rant upon the European stage and to assert that might is right. Democracy is in dispute. It flabbily yields to threatened force, gives up what is demanded of it, scurries away like a frightened rabbit and then in a jittery voice boasts of having won 'peace in our time.' Unless democracy can get up courage to fight for its liberties, which were originally won by fighting, its career seems doomed to an early end.[24]

Throughout these years, he was vocal in many quarters about fighting for liberties "just as our forefathers have done." With the bombing of Pearl Harbor in 1941, students enrolled in his philosophy class were angry, scared, and confused. One such student, Lorraine Flint, vividly remembers the fear and that he found the words to help her. Exactly which, she does not remember; but his calm demeanor and meaning that sometimes war is necessary to fight tyrants to avoid worse things than war, stay with her.

In 1943, he told a group of students that he would gladly give up the relative security of his age to regain youth "even in these troubled times...."[25] He would have changed places in order to volunteer for military service. For him it was not only a simple act of patriotism, but also a sense of high duty.

In Search of Happiness

Sommerville prided himself on his ability to range across the curriculum and to integrate all that he had learned from formal study and personal experience. He wanted the same for his students. For him the goal for all learning was to think for oneself, to have choices, and to seek truth and beauty in search of personal happiness. For

Sommerville, personal joy was the only emotion worthwhile. A temper was a waste of time. One had to achieve personal happiness in order to be the social being that was part of the Divine Plan.

He once outlined four great principles which lead to happiness: 1) to keep one's health; 2) to maintain a hardy allegiance to high duty; 3) to accept and be satisfied with one's lot in life; and 4) to enjoy the wonders and beauty of nature. Of these principles, he often emphasized that all people have a part in the drama of life and that each person should be satisfied with his or her particular role because such acceptance makes that role easier to perform. A frequent speaker in chapel services on the campus, he once told the students, "We cannot all be big brass horns, but if we blow our little tin whistles we will have accomplished our purpose in life."[26]

Notes

1. One cannot help noticing that Sommerville's subtitle, "What I Believe" is the same title of an essay written by Bertrand Russell in 1925. Although both address some of the same topics, they do disagree on most issues. As examples: Russell does not believe in life after death, but Sommerville says not only that he does not know, but he says he knows whatever the case, "... it will be well."; Sommerville's view of God was more like that of James and his disciples, certainly not one shared with Russell.

2. Richard Clarke Sommerville, "As a Man Thinketh," *The Prism* 2 (February 1940): 6-7, 15-16.

3. William Lowe Bryan, a professor of Greek and philosophy, received his Ph.D. from Clark in psychology in 1892. In 1903, he was president of the American Psychological Association. From 1902 until his retirement, he was the president of Indiana University. He conducted research in psychology and published books in the history of philosophy.

4. Students from the early thirties also reported many of the readings as being on their lists, although he had more of a tendency to adopt standard textbooks in his courses in those years.

5. Calkins completed all the work for her doctorate in psychology from Harvard in 1895. Since she was a woman, Harvard refused her the degree. She was later president of both the American Philosophical Association (1918) and the American Psychological Association (1905). In addition to her successful text listed above, she wrote textbooks in psychology and focused her studies on the study of the self. (Hilgard, 1987, p. 508) Although her work was controversial, Sommerville followed her work on self-psychology.

6. Mary W. Calkins, *The Persistent Problems of Philosophy* (New York: Macmillan 1925) Chapter 1; Charles Dunbar Broad, "Introduction," *Scientific Thought* (New York: Harcourt, Brace and Company 1923), 11-25.

7. Henri Bergson, *Matter and Memory* (New York: The Macmillan Company 1929), 299-332.

8. Bertrand Russell *The A B C of Atoms* (New York: E.P Dutton 1923), Chapters 1-4; Sir James Jeans, "The Earth," *Through Space and Time* (New York: The Macmillan Co. 1934), 1-47; William L. Bryan, *War of Families of Minds* (London: The Oxford Press 1940), Chapter 2; A. N. Whitehead, *Science and the Modern World* (New York: The Macmillan Company 1925), Chapter IX; A.S. Eddington, "Man's Place in the Universe," and "The Sidereal Universe," *The Nature of the Physical World* (New York: The Macmillan Company 1929), Chapters 1 and 8; C.L. Morgan, "Emergence," *Emergent Evolution* (New York: Henry Holt and Company 1928), Chapter 1; A.S. Eddington, "The Fitzgerald Contraction," and "Relativity," *Space, Time and Gravitation* (Cambridge: The University Press 1923), Chapters 1 and 2; J.S. Haldane, *The Philosophy of a Biologist* (Oxford: The Clarendon Press 1935), Chapter 1; Bertrand Russell, *The Problems of Philosophy* (London: The Oxford Press 1912), Chapters 1 and 2; William McDougall, "Emergent Evolution," *Modern Materialism and Emergent Evolution* (New York: Van Nostrand Co. 1929), Chapter 5; Friedrich Paulson, *Introduction to Philosophy* (Henry Holt and Co. 1930), 1-50; W.S. Hocking, "Why the Mind Needs a Body," *The Self Its Body and Freedom* (New Haven: The Yale University Press

1928), Chapter 2.

9. Ernest Thompson, *History of the Presbyterians in the South, I* (Richmond: John Knox Press 1973), 320-334.

10. Richard Clarke Sommerville, "Faculty Hob-Nobs," *The Prism,* (January 1939): 7, 16.

11. Although born into a strict and practicing Presbyterian family, there are no records of his having been baptized as a child at either Nineveh or in Moorefield. There is a record of a transfer of membership to the Old Stone Church in Lewisburg, West Virginia. Church records at Westminster Presbyterian do indicate that he transferred his membership from the First Presbyterian Church in Memphis. I was unable to track from there.

12. Richard Clarke Cabot, *What Men Live By* (Houghton Mifflin Company 1929), Chapters 10-13.; William James, *The Variety of Religious Experience* (New York: The Modern Library 1936), 430-457.

13. C. Lloyd Morgan, 11.

14. William McDougall, although subscribing to the view of emergent evolution, found much with which to disagree in Morgan's theory of emergent evolution, on rather technical terms, and so, his writings were included for balance and for little other reason. William McDougall was a physiological psychologist, trained in England and transplanted to Harvard and Duke. He espoused the Lamarckian view of evolution and attempted to prove it experimentally but failed. Although a prolific writer on many subjects, he had little following among American psychologists. Sommerville cared very little for his work for the same reason that he did not care for Freud's theories; they both emphasized that man is ruled by instincts. Sommerville, on the other hand, believed and taught that all people are basically motivated by their quest for self-perfection.

15. Francis Edward Younghusband, "An Explorer's Religion," *Atlantic Monthly (158;* December 1936): 651-655.

16. John William Navin Sullivan, "The Revolution in Science," *Atlantic Monthly (151*: March 1933): 286-94.

17. David Hume, *A Treatise on Human Nature* (Oxford: Clarendon Press 1896), 22-53.

18. William James, *Pragmatism* (London: Longmans, Green 1913), 43-85.

19. Rene Descartes, "Meditations on First Philosophy," (1641), in E. S. Haldane, ed., *The Philosophical Works of Descartes* (Cambridge: The University Press 1911-12), 88-126.

20. "Zeno of Elea," *Encyclopedia Britannica* (The exact edition is not referenced).

21. Although Zeno's paradoxes were placed much later on the reading list, they were obviously included and meant to be linked with the particular selection by David Hume. He used Zeno's paradox to argue his ideas on the divisibility of space and time. In Sommerville's course description he said that his goal was to show the student "the outstanding problems which have held the attention of thoughtful men from the beginning of reflective thinking in Greece to the present day." By linking these two passages as well as others, he did so quite effectively.

22. Henri Bergson, *An Introduction to Metaphysics.* Translated by T.E. Holme (New York: G.P. Putnam's Sons 1912), 1-32.

23. William E. Hocking, *The Meaning of God in Human Experience* (New Haven: The Yale University Press 1912), Chapters 17-20; Ralph B. Perry *Present Philosophical Tendencies* (New York: Longmans, Green and Co. 1938), Chapter 6; Plato, *Phaedo*, 149-179 (the exact publisher and edition is not referenced); I. Kant, "Theory of Ethics". In *Kant Selections.* (New York: Charles Scribers' Sons c1929); and Clarence I. Lewis, *Mind and the World-Order* (New York: Dover Publications 1929), 154-181.

24. Richard Clarke Sommerville, "Faculty Hob-Nobs," *The Prism*, (January 1939): 7, 16.

25. "Plato - Uranians Hold Annual Banquet," *The Critograph* (*29*, 7 February 11, 1943): 7.

26. *The Critograph*, (Wed., Nov. 7, 1934): 2.

7

THE PROFESSIONAL AND THE EMPLOYEE

Sommerville's contributions as an educator were not limited to the classroom. In his days of teaching, faculty members also worked on committees which oversaw all facets of college life. Today, although most of this committee work would be done by full-time staff or administrators, much of it is still the province of the faculty. For professors like Sommerville with many years of administrative experience, this committee service afforded him the opportunity to demonstrate academic, administrative, and social acumen. Here Sommerville interacted with other faculty and administrators and gained the reputation for being fair, deliberate, even-handed, and wise.

At this point Sommerville had played every defined role—student, teacher, secondary school principal, college president, graduate student, dean, professor, and finally, department chairman and division head. He was able to lead or follow, and to accept the duties of each role. As chairman of the Department of Psychology and Education, he was placed automatically on the Curriculum and Classification Committee. Here matters pertaining to the curriculum were deliberated before being passed on to the meetings of the General Faculty for action. Other committee duties included placing students in programs, making any exemptions or exceptions to program requirements, and evaluating transfer credits. In 1932, following a departmental reorganization into divisions, Sommerville was named head of the Division of Psychology and Education. When a Faculty Council, also known as the Executive Committee of the Faculty, was created, he was automatically a member, a position that he held until his retirement in 1946. The Faculty Council, the most powerful group on the campus, deliberated matters concerning admissions, curriculum, social policies, and academic life before they were sent on to the meetings of the General Faculty for ratification.

Sommerville's other duties included the Library Committee where decisions were made about professional journal and book selections and resource allocation. Additionally, he was often on the Catalogue Committee which compiled and edited *The Bulletin of Lynchburg College* and the Religious Activities Committee which arranged the compulsory chapel services. The Research Committee which served various purposes from encouraging faculty research to gathering data about research activity, also claimed his attention. He was regularly appointed to other standing committees such as those concerned with freshmen orientation and the campus lectures and fine arts series. He was the faculty advisor to the student government, the *Critograph*, the student newspaper, and the *Prism*, the student literary magazine. In most years he was assigned to as many as four, five, or six of the standing committees, not counting the many *Ad Hoc* committees appointed by the dean, the president, and/

or the board of trustees, particularly during the depression years.

The Faculty Pay the Price

During the depression years, Dr. Sommerville not only adjusted his program, but also suffered financial difficulties, a situation he could not have foreseen when he signed his contract in 1928. In the late twenties, optimism swept the country, the state, and Lynchburg as everyone expected prosperity. Herbert Hoover had been elected with the promise of "a chicken in every pot and two cars in every garage." Moreover, farm reform was in the offing. The stock market was providing its investors with real and imaginary wealth and real estate was over-valued. Because the fledgling Lynchburg College was too new to have amassed a cushion to absorb the blows of the depression years, the stock market crash of 1929 immediately affected the college.

The faculty and staff, while attending to the everyday academic issues, were painfully aware of the financial situation. Throughout the worst years of the depression, they worked without a tenure policy or a pension plan. In some months they also taught without pay and when payment was made, it was often for less than the contracted amount. Within a year of the crash, the college announced a plan to raise money for the general operations fund. A maintenance drive was launched as an emergency campaign. A committee comprised of faculty, administrators, and trustees, of which Sommerville was a member, was appointed to oversee the campaign. The faculty were asked to make voluntary donations, as much as they could afford. Although three-fourths of the goal was raised in seven months, the end of the year brought the news that faculty salaries would be cut by ten percent.[1]

Since the campaign met with little success from the outside, the 1931-32 academic year was a busy one as the college streamlined programs and further cut expenses. Sommerville was asked to chair a special five-member committee to look at intercollegiate sports, as the athletic program was operating at a deficit. All quarters of the campus were polled so that the committee had maximum input. It recommended that intercollegiate football be eliminated because it was too expensive to operate. While the college gave no athletic scholarships as such, it did fund quite a few "athletic assistants." The faculty also reasoned that student conduct could be improved without football. The faculty accepted the recommendation of the committee and football has never returned to the campus to this day. However, members of the trustees asked that football be reconsidered in 1937. At that time Sommerville read an abstract from the special Athletic Committee's report, as originally presented on May 6, 1932, and the faculty adopted a formal resolution not to restore football. They saw its impact on student conduct as a step backward![2]

During these years, the faculty received contracts but sometimes were also assessed a "donation" which meant that when salaries were made, they were often for less than the contracted amount. As time wore on, the faculty were not being paid, sometimes as long as two and a half months.[3] As well, the assessed "donation" meant that the faculty were being taxed on money that they had not received. When the contracts were let for the 1934-35 academic year and the faculty were again asked for the "donation," Sommerville sent a letter accepting his contract for the 1934-35 session and agreed to having his salary reduced by the $175.00 as requested. However, he did not agree to calling it a "donation." His first reason was based on the income tax laws where both federal and state regulations allowed only fifteen percent exemption for charitable donations. Since such a sum would put him over the limit, and he was not only taxed on what he had not received, but also prevented from benefitting by the tax laws. His second reason reflected his opinion that the action of the trustees in February, in fact, was a reduction of faculty salaries. Here he was referring to an action by the board in February, 1933, which let contracts for the next year at a stated sum, but later added a troublesome phrase, "subject to whatever deductions or cuts the necessities of the administration may deem necessary to avoid a deficit."[4] He further argued that as he already owned money to other groups in pledges, he could not afford to make such a large contribution. Sommerville avowed his loyalty to the college, said it was welcome to the money, but demanded that the "donation" be called a reduction.[5]

In terms of real moneys, the faculty had paid dearly, perhaps some more heavily than others. According to Orville Wake,

At the close of the fiscal year in June 1928, the highest salary was $3,000, the lowest $1,200, and the average $2,491. In 1934-35, the highest teacher's salary was $2,500, the lowest $1,600, and the average was $2,108.[6]

How others fared is not known, but on April 4, 1936, Sommerville wrote a letter to the president acknowledging receipt of his contract. He agreed to the stated salary of $2,350.00 and thanked him for the increase in salary![7] Sommerville had started at the salary of $3,000 per year, set for all department chairmen. In 1936, even though Sommerville had remained chairman of the Division of Psychology and Education, his salary was below the maximum salary for 1934. He had seen his salary drop steadily over his then eight years of service.

Sommerville probably did not worry much about money unless he felt that he might not meet his financial obligations. However, he was always concerned about fairness and good faith. In 1935, the faculty had not received contracts, so he and the dean were asked to draw up a resolution expressing the feelings of the faculty concerning the delay. The resolution passed unanimously. At this time, and for the second time, he asked that the issue of permanent tenure for the faculty be considered.[8] The delay this time was caused primarily because the executive committee of the board of trustees was in the process of working out a new system to retire all debts and begin a new fund raising drive. This plan did eventually work during which time there were many morale boosting changes for the faculty, such as a retirement plan, a tenure system, and plans to cover all back pay.

After Sommerville received tenure in 1937, a pension plan was adopted in 1938. Ironically, he wrote a letter thanking the president for his contract that year and expressing appreciation for the greater security provided him by the tenure system. While he may have perceived it as greater security in 1937 at the age of sixty-two, the system called for a mandatory retirement age, one that Dr. Sommerville would not welcome in nine years. It is interesting to note that at the time of his retirement in 1946, his final year's salary was $2900.[9]

Although Sommerville seemed to be a special victim of the depression years, in fact, he was in better shape than many, particularly the new young faculty members who had no savings, and who were trying to begin the transition from graduate student, where poverty is a way of life, to faculty status where a much different life style is required. Dr. Sommerville had spent a life time coping with financial and medical uncertainty. Over the years he had managed to obtain an education through the master's level during the depression of the eighteen-eighties and nineties. The trek out west with little, and finally no money, where his death was assumed, had challenged his resolve to survive. Many times in his life he had started over when his health would not allow him to continue with successful pursuits. During these years, however, he was remarkably in good health, even considered robust, thanks in part to the development of antibiotics. He lived frugally all his life always with a view of saving for a rainy day; this helped him to survive during lean years.

He was also relatively secure in his position. While others lost their jobs or chose to move on to other professions, his position was secure as there were only two ways for him to go—either voluntarily or for the school to close. If he worried about the latter, there is no record of it nor any way to attribute such concerns to him. Rather, during these challenging times he carved out quite a niche in Lynchburg, establishing himself both personally and professionally.

Some Traditions Begin

Throughout the depression years, the faculty were not only expected keep the students focused on academics; they were called upon not to discuss the financial situation with anyone because this might further complicate the recruiting process. As recruiters in the field attempted to attract students for the coming year in the summer of 1932, they received criticism from both parents and towns people about student conduct on and off the campus. There was a general sentiment among some that the campus was a party school and that the students did not take their studies seriously. Actually by today's standards for tolerance, the student conduct was not that bad. But these were depression years, and there was little tolerance for anyone appearing to behave frivolously in these hard times. An eleven-member faculty committee was appointed to look into these concerns and to develop a code of conduct for students. Sommerville was chair of a five-member committee concerned with the latter issue which drew up a pledge of cooperation which all students had to sign upon matriculation, a practice that continued for many years.[10]

Out of these introspective exercises came the Student Honor Code and a revamping of the Men's and Women's Councils with a view to encourage more self-governance on the part of the student. The college mirrored the national trend away from paternalistic governance and toward more self-reliance—a trend which was to become a tradition at Lynchburg College as well as on other college campuses.

Although Sommerville served with loyalty at all times he did not hesitate to speak out on issues not to his liking even if he had been part of the mistake. Following notification that the Southern Association would make a site visit as part of the college accreditation self-study, he was placed on the trustee-appointed Curriculum Committee which came up with the idea of moving from the semester system to the quarter system.[11] Several financial and academic reasons for the quarter system. During this time the college had entered into a formal agreement with Virginia Polytechnic Institute (VPI) in Blacksburg for pre-engineering students to begin studies at Lynchburg for two years and then transfer to VPI in order to complete the engineering program. The Curriculum Committee thought that the college should switch to the quarter system so that students could more easily articulate between the two schools.

The second reason was to improve teaching and learning. The three-hour courses were all turned into five-hour courses because the faculty determined that the same amount of material had to be covered in the quarter system as in the semester system. Thus the students and the teachers had to spend longer hours in the classroom for a shorter period of time. Additionally, faculty had yet another set of final exams to grade, adding more work for all involved.

Sommerville prepared and delivered a stinging critique of the system, although he had served on the committee which initiated the idea. He had actually made the motion in the faculty meeting to go on the quarter system. Calling forth the literature on the nature of learning and retention in spaced and un-spaced practice, he concluded that spaced learning was best because it allowed for reflection. Sommerville further studied the performance of students in his classes under both systems, comparing earned grades with student performance on abilities tests (all students had to take abilities tests in those days). He concluded that student learning under the quarter system was not improved, and if anything, was the same or poorer. He further objected to having to teach for longer hours and to conduct beginning courses every quarter. A few days later, at a meeting of the Faculty Council it was decided to explore how others felt about the system. Since it was unpopular with everyone, the faculty decided to reinstate the semester system the next academic year.[12]

The Student-Teacher Relationship

A second facet of the quarter system was to have included a distinction between the junior college (liberal studies) and the senior college (studies in the major). Sommerville had chaired a sub-committee of two, himself and the dean, to come up with a plan to accomplish this

Richard Sommerville in the 1940's
(COURTESY OF LYNCHBURG COLLEGE ARCHIVES —
VIRGINIA DUNN, ARCHIVIST)

distinction. The proposed report revealed Sommerville's goals of education and the role of the student-teacher. Essentially, it would require qualifying examinations across the curriculum after the first two years of study and before the student could matriculate into the senior college. In the senior college, the student would take a prescribed sequence of course work, but could audit any course without extra payment. At the end of the two years of study, the student would take comprehensive examinations in an area of concentration. Performance on this examination would determine graduation, not grades. Grades were to be used as progress reports. All upper level courses would become seminars, rather than set class hours.

The primary goals of such a program were five:

1. The distant goal motivates the student during the upper years and forces him to retain, review, read, think in broad patterns. 2. Outside examining raises the tone of instruction. 3. Outside examining stimulates scholarship in instructors as well as in students. 4. Outside examining develops cooperation between students and professors. 5. Outside examining adds greatly to the dignity of the student's degree.[13]

The committee report said that aside from the potential loss of the poorer students, the cost of the senior exam alone would be over one thousand dollars a year. The report was submitted to the General Faculty but it was never accepted. At first it was tabled until a special call meeting was held to deal specifically with the proposal. At that time it was sent back to the committee for reconsideration as sentiment was so strongly against it. The proposal was never returned to the faculty again, a point that Sommerville carped about in his critique of the quarter system.[14]

Sommerville worked for over a year on the idea of the outside exams and was a strong advocate of this particular model which was common in some institutions at the time, especially at large universities such as Chicago and Columbia. While it might, as some had feared, have led to the loss of students, it certainly had the potential to raise standards as the report suggested. Moreover, it was in keeping with Sommerville's style of teaching which was to provide reading lists along with or in lieu of textbooks. He expected students to study on their own, writing weekly reports which were turned in for evaluation, in addition to the regularly scheduled tests and exams. He saw the classroom as the opportunity to engage in debate and/or drill in some classes; he used the lecture to integrate, synthesize, and augment the assigned material.

His proposed system reflected his view of the college professor and his or her role with the student. Under this system, the professor and the student become allies in learning the material because they focus on the common goal of the examinations, which become all important in receiving the degree. As the examinations are set by some outside source, the teacher-student relationship itself is never adversarial, but is a shared learning experience. Grades, or "marks" as he called them, may be given as progress reports, not as final grades which are then added, multiplied, and divided to create some sort of cumulated grade point average used to rank students. The shared-learning model ultimately places the responsibility on the student to actively participate in his or her learning, focusing attention on strengths and weakness, and allowing the student to look for classes to improve weaknesses without penalty. The teacher-as-the-final-arbiter-of-grades model ultimately reduces the student's responsibility, since the student perceives the teacher as the only person who must be impressed. Weaknesses must never be admitted because there is a penalty for so doing. The rule then becomes, "don't take classes where one is

weak because they will ruin the grade point average."
Sommerville hated this view of college teaching.

A New Set of Challenges

The war years of the late thirties and forties were to
present a different set of challenges. Whereas, during the
depression, the college had students but no money, the
forties brought a retirement of debt but fewer students.
According to Dr. Wake's account,

> After the outbreak of the war in Europe, employment oppor-
> tunities became more generally available to youth of the college
> age and this had an effect upon the enrollment of the College.
> As the international tensions mounted, the National Guard was
> called into service, the Selective Service system was put into
> operation, and after Pearl Harbor large numbers of young men
> were called into the armed services. This resulted in a decrease
> in the enrollment of regular students at Lynchburg College
> from 277 in 1938-39 to 142 in 1943-44. Had it not been for other
> developments that took place in the meantime, the financial
> consequences of this decrease in enrollment would have been
> devastating.[15]

These "other developments" included the use of
the campus for several military training programs which
required the housing and teaching of large groups of young
men on the campus and in cooperation with the community. During these years, there were flight training programs for the Army Air Force and the Navy Cross Country
Flight group, both in cooperation with the Civil Aeronau-
tics Authority. The largest group was the 14th Army Air
Force Training Detachment which brought 560 Army Air
Corps cadets in fourteen months from March 21, 1943 to
May 4, 1944.[16]

The challenges before the school included rearranging programs, providing faculty for both the military programs and the civilian liberal arts program, and finding ways to coordinate both peacefully. According to Dr. Wake, community and college groups were in conflict over the military presence on the campus which, "created uneasiness in the soul of the campus."[17] There is no question how one faculty member, Richard Sommerville, felt about the military presence. His long ingrained sense of patriotism led him to much support of all the college's efforts. Available minutes of the Executive Committee of the Faculty do not reflect conflict but do reflect the work of a seasoned set of players, each executing his or her respective duties in the setting of the day. Sommerville was somewhat active in finding solutions to the tough problems.

One solution to the challenges presented because of the war was the initiation of summer school which allowed men and women to finish their degree programs in three years. Summer school classes have been held ever since. Other solutions to the uncertainty created by the draft included giving professors more flexibility in working with the individual student. Some of the policies prevail to this day.[18]

Sommerville's professional life was not limited to the campus and the classroom. His interests included involvement in professional organizations concerned with promoting scholarship in subject areas of interest to him. Shortly after his arrival in Virginia, he was accepted to membership in the Virginia Academy of Sciences and served as secretary of the Psychology Division from 1934-36. He regularly attended the annual meetings and remained active all his professional life. He joined and or managed to maintain membership in the American Psychological Association, the Southern Society of Philosophy and Psychology, The American Association for the

Advancement of Science, and Sigma Xi. He was known to attend regional and national meetings of these organizations. From the time that Sommerville arrived on the campus until the day he retired in 1946, the college was faced with adversity. Always the loyal employee, Sommerville was never afraid to do what he thought best. While he may not always have been right, he was willing to take a personal stand on issues. Throughout these tough times, he created a life for himself and left a lasting legacy. Equally adept in the classroom, in the committee meeting, or in an administrative office, Sommerville was at home in academia.

Notes

1. *Minutes of the Faculty*, November 11, 1930; *Minutes of the Board of Trustees*, June 8, 1931; March 4, 1932.

2. *Minutes of the Faculty*, May 3, 1937.

3. *Minutes of the Trustees*, February 21, 1933.

4. *Minutes of the Faculty*, February 25, 1933.

5. Letter, Richard Sommerville to President J.T.T. Hundley, 5 March 1934.

6. Orville Wake, "The History of Lynchburg College, 1903-1953," (Unpublished doctoral dissertation, 1957), 233.

7. Letter, Richard Sommerville to R.B. Montgomery, 4 April 1936.

8. *Minutes of the Faculty*, March 15, 1934; May 17, 1935.

9. Letter, R.B. Montgomery to R.C. Sommerville, 13 March 1945.

10. *Minutes of the Faculty*, May 6, 1932.

11. Curriculum Committee of the Board, *Minutes of the Trustees*, June 4, 1934.

12. *Minutes of the Faculty,* February 1 and March 8, 1937; *Minutes of the Faculty Council*, February 4, 23; March 2, 1937.

13. *Minutes of the Faculty Council*, December 9, 1935.

14. *Minutes of the Faculty*, January 6, 1936.
15. Wake, 268-269.
16. Ibid., 270-271.
17. Ibid., 269.
18. *Minutes of the Executive Committee of the Faculty*, Sept. 30, 1940; January 14, 1941; Oct. 22, 1942; March 29, 1943; April 21, 1944.

8

"Friend of the Student"

O ver the years, although Sommerville's position at Lynchburg College afforded him many opportunities to utilize his many administrative skills, he is not remembered for them. Rather, his relationship with the students essentially guaranteed his legacy. His popularity with them surfaced immediately in student publications, such as annuals, newspapers, magazines, and the like. From the students' viewpoint at Arkansas College, Sommerville must have been able to cope well with his dual role of teacher-student during the years that he was also working on his doctorate at Columbia. The students dedicated the 1923 *Index*, the Arkansas College annual, to Sommerville with the following inscription:

DEDICATION
to
Mr. Richard C. Summerville (sic), A.M.
Who, as true Christian gentleman, a real scholar, a wise adviser, a friend of the student, and, above all a man who, by his splendid personality and unretiring patience, has gained the lasting

149

respect and admiration of every student of A.C., do we, the staff, to whom he has been an especial source of inspiration, dedicate this, the 1923 Index.[1]

The Dedication echoed sentiments expressed earlier by parents and colleagues in letters of reference for Richard Sommerville, both as a person and as a scholar. Phrases, such as "friend of the student," "unretiring patience," "a wise adviser," and "lasting respect and admiration of every student," were to become his legacy. The Dedication foretold his relationship with the students at Lynchburg College years later. Interestingly, at the time of the Dedication, Sommerville was in his mid-forties. By the time that he began teaching at Lynchburg College, he was into his fifties, the age when one might expect to find a "generation gap," a phrase popularized in the media in the nineteen-seventies. However, such a gap never existed between Sommerville and his students.

Moreover, when the college students spoke for themselves, they never made any reference to his having been a strict disciplinarian. This characterization had been emphasized in both his letters of reference and in the local newspaper accounts of his presidency of the Lewisburg Seminary for Girls. Obviously, Sommerville mellowed with age. Once when he was in his late seventies or early eighties, he was having a conversation with his student and later good friend, Lavelon Sydnor. Mr. Sydnor interrupted their conversation to discipline his children for making too much noise while playing in the yard. Sommerville interrupted him and told him to "let the children play, laugh, and make noise." He remarked that in his youth, he had been a strong disciplinarian, and perhaps was at one time too strict with children, but no more.[2]

In 1942, echoing sentiments that had been expressed by students at Arkansas College in 1923, the staff of the *Argonaut* dedicated their yearbook to him. The Dedication indicates that Sommerville's students clearly understood his goals for teaching and his educational philosophy.

TO
RICHARD CLARKE SOMMERVILLE

In appreciation of his years of devoted service at Lynchburg College, and in recognition of his profound scholarship, and his keen insight into the deeper realities of life. A 'lover of wisdom' who has long served the ideals of the true, the good, and the beautiful, he seeks to stimulate his students to construct for themselves a well-balanced philosophy of life. We, the students of L.C., are proud to claim him, a man of undoubted genius, as our true friend.

Although Sommerville believed that all education should have utility, in his later years, he especially emphasized that teaching should lead the student to self understanding. Further, the student should know where he or she stands on important issues. The role of the teacher is not simply to teach disjointed facts, but to integrate the material into cohesive wholes. The student's role is to learn the material, not as an end, but as a means for learning about the world and one's place in it. To this end, Sommerville assigned the students the task of writing about their views. From the tribute in *The Argonaut*, the students knew clearly what he stood for and why he gave the assignment. Also, as did the students in Arkansas, the students at Lynchburg College thought of him as their "true friend."

In 1971, a former student and later colleague, Dr. Mervyn Williamson, was commissioned to write an article about Richard Sommerville which appeared in the *Lynchburg College Magazine*. He, too, was apparently struck by the consistency of opinions:

Although hundreds of Lynchburg College alumni have their own personal recollections of Dr. Sommerville with perhaps as many differences, there is surprising agreement on his general characteristics. In the minds of most of his associates he was a living example of a "scholar and gentleman." A man of great dignity, rather reserved, he was always even-tempered, courteous, urbane, witty, pleasant in conversation, methodical in his habits, a good companion with an unusually large store of knowledge. He did not hesitate to introduce into his courses relevant allusions to other fields of knowledge, and he seemed conversant with an unusually large number of them. He knew science and mathematics widely and profoundly; he was an expert in anatomy and physiology; and he read Greek for pleasure. He liked to explore relationships among the various fields of humane learning.[3]

With the passage of some forty to fifty years, his former students still remember him fondly and with a respectful confidence in his academic ability, his kindness, and his sense of humor. One compelling account came from William Shackelford who said if students ever asked questions in the classroom, Dr. Sommerville would take his time to answer. "He would stare out the window of the classroom which was Hopwood 23. In that long pause I was confident that he was reviewing for the appropriate answer and in that time he was summing up all the philosophy, all the psychology, all the science, whatever subject was relevant, to give the best answer, very deliberately and very slowly."[4] He went on to add that if a student ever wanted a quick answer, he would not get it from Dr. Sommerville. Many would grow impatient with his extended pauses, and his style did not suit everyone.

His students tended to disagree on whether or not he was a good classroom teacher. Some expressed disappointment over his teaching style, especially the use of workbooks in some classes which were called "crib" courses, while others described lively class debates, especially in the philosophy classes. Sommerville had a habit of assigning workbooks in the psychology classes. In those days workbooks were not as common as they are today. He not only required the students to buy them, but he also insisted that they answer and submit for grading all study questions. This practice was not popular with some of his students as they thought it trivialized his classes. Some said that he was a hard marker. Decipherable data on his grading tends to bear this out. His grades almost always followed the "normal curve" and his marks were lower compared to those of most other faculty.

Sommerville is remembered for being a "very forward thinker" and as being, in many instances, a "man ahead of his time." He was known not to shy away from predicting political and social events with remarkable accuracy. Mr. Stanley Jordan remembered being influenced by a lecture on child-rearing and wrote a paper in the nineteen-thirties about the need for parents to allow children to make more decisions for themselves. His concern was that the autocratic parenting style left children unable to make decisions for themselves. He also thought this an appropriate area of research and that parenting was a good area for training. Dr. Sommerville gave him an A+ on his paper and told him that he was fifty years ahead of his time. "Sure enough!" said Jordan in the summer of 1983, "We have books about child rearing and parenting classes everywhere!"[5]

Perhaps Sommerville's most profound impact came not from the classroom, but in his interactions with the students elsewhere on the campus, as he was seen as very supportive with his heavy involvement in all campus activities. He could be found in Professor Georgia Morgan's art studio painting alongside the students or giving invited presentations at one of the literary societies. For a very few, however, there were the long talks at home with him in his garden. Over the years at 307 Vernon Street a small garden had been tilled and styled with hedges, flowers, shrubs, and fruit trees. This garden was his setting for entertaining visitors, and it provided others with lasting memories of him.

Dr. Sommerville did not generally invite students into his home as was the custom of many of the professors of his day. However, there were exceptions. One such student was Stuart Bruchey who studied for two years at Lynchburg College before transferring to major in economics at Johns Hopkins University. He was later to become the Nevins Scholar at Columbia University for Economic History. At the end of two years of study, during which time he had developed an especially close friendship with Dr. Sommerville, he told his mentor that he was going to transfer because he did not think he could learn more in his chosen field unless he did. Sommerville called him a "wise fool" and then not only agreed that his student should transfer, but also helped him to do so. For more than ten years, Bruchey was to return to see Sommerville annually, hitchhiking, if necessary. They spent countless hours in the garden or walking and talking on a wide range of subjects. When his own life made regular visits impossible, they corresponded on a regular basis until Sommerville's death. "He was my beloved master and I was his devoted student."[6]

Known as the "brilliant conversationalist," Sommerville spent long hours with another student, Phillips Freer:

> How well I do remember Dr. Sommerville the person; he was certainly a gentle man. His main influence on me, which was great, did not occur in the classroom, but was the result of many evenings talking with him in the back yard of his small house. I do not remember him as being a particularly inspiring lecturer, but he was certainly an inspiring conversationalist. He

sparked my intellectual awakening! Several times in my conversations with him at his house or in the back yard, we talked
about Freudian Psychology. I was a Freudian (still am) but Dr.
Sommerville was not sure that he approved of Freud.[7]

While Sommerville is remembered for his store of
knowledge and his eagerness to share it, his gentlemanly
ways, and his deep spirituality, he had a lighter side. Many
remember various Sommerville antics. He usually exhibited a dry sense of humor and was capable of putting
people on. He loved to tell stories. Although his class-
rooms were usually formal, he would take time out for
relating personal experiences, such as the time he was
invited to a Halloween costume party on Rivermont
Avenue. Sommerville, according to Dr. Alan Stanger,
dressed either as Cyrano de Bergerac or the Pied Piper (he
could not remember which) and boarded the trolley, for-
getting the address at home. He traveled in costume until
he saw a place that looked right because cars were parked
outside and other people were dressed for the occasion. He
went inside, never recognized anyone nor removed his
mask. Reporting to his students about his "marvelous
time," when asked how he knew it was the party he was
supposed to attend, he confessed that he did not know and
dramatically outstretched his hands, tilting his head upward, saying: "I just love a gooood Pardy!"[8]

Just as they could remember stories told by him,
many had stories and memories of their own; some still
like to do Sommerville imitations, seldom perceived with
malice, and all appear to indicate that his students were
comfortable with him. For many, a trip to Lynchburg after
graduation, always included a visit to see Dr. Sommerville
either in his classroom or at his home. It appears that he
earned the accolade, "friend of the student," not only for
his willingness to listen to their personal problems and

give advice on occasion, but also for his eagerness to chat about any topic of interest to them, and to share their lives. "I simply loved the man. I studied hard because I had such respect for him; I did not want to disappoint him." Such were the sentiments as expressed by Mrs. Lorraine Flint. Similar statements of respect were expressed by others who studied with him.

More than a friend and a teacher, Sommerville was a symbol. In 1983, on the occasion of the fiftieth class reunion of the Class of 1933, a gentleman was listening intently to the discussions that a small group was having on what and how Sommerville taught. Anecdotes were being exchanged. After listening patiently for a few minutes, he said: "It was not so much what he taught, what he did, or what he said. He was a symbol of what we could become if we plied ourselves to our studies. We were poor boys from the country; you see, he was our model." Then he disappeared into the larger group.[9]

Dr. Sommerville made friends very easily although he was always very formal with most people. Ever the pleasant conversationalist, he was never one to pry, gossip, or talk much about himself unless asked a direct question. Like many people who are as self-contained, he had many acquaintances whom he had met through collegiate and community involvements, but very few truly intimate friends. Also like many highly educated and successful people, his friendships were intergenerational.

The closest and most enduring friendship began with the Moseleys who lived across from Sommerville's home on Vernon Street. Mrs. Moseley took a special interest in Dr. Sommerville and would certainly be recognized as a very good neighbor. She looked after him when he was ill, seeing to it that he had both food and good nursing care. Her daughter, Melva, grew up knowing Dr. Sommerville. As a child she took her dolls and toys to play in his yard and often he would join her. She sometimes was allowed in the house between four and five o'clock during weekdays. Saturdays brought the "big treat" when she would be allowed to listen to the radio; her favorite program was *The Shadow*. Sometimes she could stay long enough to listen to another program and get lunch. He would feed her Vienna sausages and crackers. Ever the teacher, he tutored her, usually in math. In later years, he also tutored her daughter Pamela.

While students at Lynchburg College, Melva met and fell in love with George Adams. One afternoon while strolling by College Lake, they stood under an oak tree and George proposed marriage. Melva accepted. As a wedding present to them, Professor Sommerville captured the setting on canvas. Now George was added to the family circle and their friendship lasted until the end of Sommerville's life. When he was incapacitated, George and Melva nursed him in their home and looked after his affairs. Following his death, George was the executor of his estate.

The Sommerville family was very grateful to the Adams' as indicated by a letter of October 7, 1956 written by Margery Hatcher, his niece, to Dr. Felix Welton. It said in part: "Just had a card from Uncle Rich telling me about having pneumonia and that Melva, the little girl who used to bring her dolls and play in his yard, now married and Mrs. George Adams, took him to her home and has nursed him carefully. What a blessing such friends are!"[10]

Sommerville's move to Lynchburg also allowed him to renew his friendship with Mr. C.A. Sydnor who had been his roommate at Hampden-Sydney. They had both become educators and had corresponded over the intervening years. The Sydnor family moved to Lynchburg from Chatham, Virginia, where Mr. Sydnor was head master of Hargrave Military Academy. They managed to get together almost every Sunday evening at the Sydnor home where Sommerville was a welcomed dinner guest. According to Lavelon Sydnor, when Sommerville visited on Sunday evening for dinner, there was a big feast; when he was absent, Sunday dinner consisted of leftovers! Over the years the Sydnor children grew up knowing Dr. Sommerville very well. Several of the five children were also his students at Lynchburg College and maintained close touch until his death.

Dr. Sommerville remained a bachelor all his life—a fact that intrigued his students and gave rise to much romantic speculation. One such story was that he was once engaged, but the young woman died, and he spent the remainder of his years pining away. According to family members, there was a young lady with whom he was attached during his student years at Hampden-Sydney and the family expected marriage, but she married another. While the details are not known because Dr. Sommerville never talked about it, some believe that she married after he was sent out West because of tuberculosis. In his later years, when he was more inclined to take personal questions, he once told Lavelon Sydnor that "the trip out West had cost him dearly." This was his only answer to the question of why he had never married. When asked why he did not find another, he said that he was "never going to get into that sort of thing again!"[11]

Sommerville liked the company of women and, in later years, many of his closest friends were women. His social adroitness and his personal charm coupled with his tendency to be a loner led him to be selective in his social relationships. He tended to socialize with people based on common interests both on and off the campus. His formal style made socializing with him easy and enjoyable.

Within the community in the early thirties, he co-founded, along with Dean Lowell McPherson, a private men's group called Club 13, so named because the membership was limited to thirteen men invited from the community. This group met monthly for fellowship, fun, and relaxation, and for discussion of literature, scientific topics, or anything of interest to the group. After graduation, many of his former students settled in Lynchburg and became part of Club 13 and, therefore, part of his circle of friends. To this day, professors from the local colleges and citizens of the community are active members of the club. Although the membership is not limited to thirteen, it is still for males only.

Always the formal man, Richard Sommerville conducted himself with pride and dignity. He had the ability to make everyone who knew him feel just a little bit special, and his students appreciated him for it. Such was his legacy, one that he carefully cultivated, and one that stills lives in the memories of those who felt privileged to be his students.

Notes

1. R.W. Wygale, Letter to Mervyn Williamson with enclosures, 7 January 1972. Williamson Papers. Lynchburg College Archives.

2. Lavelon Sydnor, Interview with author, 15 March 1983.

3. Mervyn Williamson, "Man of Many Parts," *The Lynchburg College Magazine*, (1971), 10.

4. William Shackelford, Interview with author, 11 March 1983.

5. Stanley Jordan, Interview with author, 23 March 1983.

6. Stuart Bruchey, Interview with author, 7 February 1984.

7. Letter, Phillips Freer to author, 10 September 1987.

8. Allen Stanger, Interview with author, 16 April 1983.

9. 16 April 1983.

10. Welton Family Papers.

11. Sydnor, 1983.

9

THE MAN AND HIS ART

A Lifelong Love of the Theatre

R ichard Sommerville grew up in a family that valued the visual and performing arts as a means of both socialization and recreation. By far, Sommerville devoted his greater store of energy and interests within the community to three organizations: Lynchburg Little Theatre, The Civic Art League, and the Lynchburg Art Club.

Since the end of the nineteenth century, the town had a long-established reputation for the fine arts. In 1921, The Little Theatre of Lynchburg was organized. A group of local women from the Lynchburg Women's Club held a public meeting to determine community interest in starting an amateur drama club. Eighty-five citizens of the town arrived at the Masonic Auditorium, and the idea translated almost overnight into a plan. In the first year, five plays were performed attended by over two hundred members, with over seventy of them participating in some way with the productions. By the time Sommerville arrived in 1928, membership in The Little Theatre had more than doubled. He personally witnessed its further growth to more than one thousand by the end of the nineteen-forties. From the beginning, because of the large community interest and involvement, the group could afford a professional director. Lynchburg was the first city in Virginia to build its own theatre.[1]

Probably at the encouragement of Dean Lowell McPherson and his wife, who were active members, during his first year in Lynchburg, Sommerville auditioned and secured the part of Jasper Hardy, the villain in *The Bad Man*. This play was performed on May 15-17, 1929, and "went on the road" to the city of Roanoke, Virginia, and then to Hollins College. His debut in this satirical comedy about a young man who lost his ranch located on the Mexican Border partly through his own mistakes and partly because of its location, did not go unnoticed in the local paper, *The News*: "...there was not a part last night which did not conform to the high standards of the Lynchburg Little Theatre for participants in its plays....Dr. R.C. Sommerville of Lynchburg College, going far to impress upon the audience of the cold-blooded propensities of the 'loan-feesh' whose part he took so convincingly...."[2]

His debut in this play was the beginning of an association that lasted until his death in 1963. He served on the governing board from 1936-1948 and held office as vice-president for the 1946-47 season when he was seventy-one years old. On many occasions he was a member of the casting committee which held auditions and selected the cast for plays. Sometimes eight or ten people would audition for a part, but an effort was always made to keep a balance between seasoned players and "new-comers." Over the years, he also worked with the play-reading committee which read many plays, culling the number to recommend five or six annually to the board. Care was taken to vary the entertainment, including farces, satires, melodramas, musicals, and operettas. Sommerville personally preferred the more serious productions.

For over twenty-eight years, in addition to his work on the board, Sommerville performed in many plays. Although the records are not complete, they sufficiently indicate his commitment to amateur theatre. In 1931, he played the role of Dr. Richard Gaunt in *Three Wise Fools*, and the Reverend Ernest Lynton in *Aren't We All?*. By the 1947-48 season, when he took the part of Sir Peter Teazle in *School for Scandal*, he had reportedly participated on stage in at least fifteen plays.[3]

At the age of seventy, after his retirement from Lynchburg College, he did not retire from amateur theatre. He stepped up his participation to include at least eight more plays by 1956. That year saw his last role on the stage of the Lynchburg Little Theatre, when at the age of eighty-one, he played Ramsden Briar Patch in *Man and Superman*. In 1955, he was awarded an Oscar by the members of The Little Theatre as "Best Supporting Actor" for his role as Larrabee in *Sabrina Fair*. Over the years, he did not limit his acting to the stage of the Little Theatre but performed in one-act plays for the Lynchburg Woman's Club and on stage at Lynchburg College. One of the most memorable performances was as Polonias in *Hamlet* in 1953.

Dr. Robert Hailey, who joined the faculty at Lynchburg College in 1948 as the director of the drama program, also directed The Lynchburg Little Theatre. He respected Dr. Sommerville as a person, a patron of the arts, and an amateur actor. Dr. Hailey found working with Richard Sommerville easy because he "never had to teach him about his character." Sommerville "always knew his role and he always knew his lines." Moreover, Richard understood the plays and was very cooperative with the director on interpretation. For Dr. Hailey, "Richard Sommerville brought more to the stage than a knowledge of character and line, he brought depth, warmth, and a sincere commitment to amateur theatre as it is supposed to be."[4]

Sommerville's sense of personal dignity, his intellect, and his sense of humor, left a lasting impression with Robert Hailey. But the scene that sticks in Dr. Hailey's memory most vividly demonstrated Sommerville's tendency to ignore his age. Richard Sommerville often boasted: "Years make the body old and tired, but not Richard Sommerville's." During a rehearsal of *Hamlet*, a student was to play the role of an aging man but his gait did not suit Dr. Sommerville. "Here's how I would walk if I were playing the part of an old man," he told the student. Dr. Hailey turned around to see the nearly eighty-year-old man limp across the stage!

Likewise, he is remembered by Mrs. Polly Payne as being a "gentle, delightful person, soft-spoken, somewhat retiring, and yet a strong person."[5] According to Mrs. Payne, who designed the stage sets for the plays and served on the board with Dr. Sommerville, he had a great depth of interpreting, never overplayed his part, took his acting seriously, and obviously loved the theatre.

According to Dr. Hailey, Mrs. Payne, and others, the key in Dr. Sommerville's work in the theatre was a commitment to the group and to the theatre. He served loyally, with keen interest and good cheer. His interests were not limited to those of actor, reader, or committee chairman; he was also a devoted patron.

"Academic Realism"

From a very early age Sommerville enjoyed painting and drawing. His mother and his sisters were his first teachers and, as recorded earlier, he had been the protégé of Will Alexander who specialized in painting horses. Sommerville had also taken a course in drawing at the preparatory school at Hampden-Sydney College. He probably did not study art formally again until he moved to Lynchburg, although he once told some students that he attended art classes held at some of the art galleries while he was a graduate student at Columbia University in New York City.[6]

After moving to Lynchburg, he was a special student of Professor Georgia Morgan who was head of the Department of Art at Lynchburg College.[7] A well-respected artist in her own right, Miss Morgan was actively involved with two groups in town, The Lynchburg Civic Art League and the Lynchburg Art League. The former organization was founded in 1932 under the leadership of Professor Morgan and was open to all residents of the community who were at least sixteen years of age.[8] The annual shows were not judged and anyone could exhibit.

However, the Lynchburg Art League limited its membership to twenty outstanding local artists. Each had to be invited by the group as openings became available. Exhibits by this group were judged, critiqued by members and by outside experts. Miss Morgan, and her successor at Lynchburg College, Pierre Daura, were among the gifted well-known artists as was Bernhard Gutmann, of Randolph Macon Woman's College, the first art teacher in the Lynchburg Public Schools.[9] In 1944, when the membership was extended to twenty-five, Sommerville was added as a member. In 1948 he served as president.[10]

Besides his studies with Professor Morgan, Sommerville studied at the University of Virginia and the Pennsylvania Academy, and took private lessons with Eliot Clarke, a nationally recognized painter, teacher, lecturer, and writer.[11] Among his many affiliations, Clarke was a member of the National Art Club, New York City, as well as the Art Clubs of Connecticut, Savannah, Georgia, and Lynchburg.[12] In 1935, he was in Lynchburg working with the Art Club as a teacher and critic and giving public lectures.[13] It is probable that they knew each other before their Lynchburg years.

In the mid-thirties, Sommerville began exhibiting his paintings. His first exhibit was in November of 1935, at the Fourth Annual Exhibition, held at 506 Main Street. There were four oil paintings titled, *Study in Blue and Brown*, *Blue Jar*, *The End of Autumn*, and *Pennsylvanian Hills*.[14] The annual exhibitions displayed the talents of the area artists to sell their works. Sommerville's paintings were exhibited and they sold. It is impossible to track ownership or even to know how many he painted, but he did exhibit nearly every year. One of his paintings, *Barn* was selected for a special showing by the Academy of Sciences and Fine Arts in Richmond at their Eighth Annual Showing in January, 1940. In June of 1942, the Lynchburg Art Club and the Civic Art League joined forces to raise money for the U.S.O. and the Chinese War Relief. At that time, two of Sommerville's paintings were auctioned: *Earthly Hope Men Set Their Hearts Upon* and *The Lake*.[15]

He is known to have exhibited other paintings throughout the years, but the records do not always list the titles, only that his work was included. The last known show in which he participated was held at E.C. Glass High School in 1956. When the Lynchburg Art Center, Inc. was founded in 1953, he was listed on the rolls of both the Art Club and the Art Center.[16] In 1955, for the occasion of the two-hundredth anniversary of the Quaker Memorial Presbyterian Church in Lynchburg, Sommerville was commissioned to design a commemorative plate of the original Quaker Meeting House built in 1757. The drawing, done in blue and printed on a white Steubenville plate, was widely sold as a fund-raising effort.

Upon his death, Mrs. George Adams compiled a list of some thirty-five major works and their owners for the family records. The records indicate that members of his family, who were the subjects of many of his paintings, retain ownership of most of these. After College Lake was created in the nineteen-thirties, along the banks he painted a series variously titled with the months of the year or with names of trees. These are listed as owned by local families and by persons as far away as Missouri, Pennsylvania, and Louisiana.

Over the years Sommerville also continued with his music. He was rather accomplished on his silver flute which he had owned since childhood and which continues to be a family heirloom. A concert grand piano, which he played rather tentatively, occupied much of one room in his home on Vernon Street in Lynchburg. As recounted earlier, while a student at Hampden-Sydney, he played the banjo and the guitar, mostly for amusement with his friends. Sommerville usually kept his music for personal relaxation, but sometimes for the enjoyment of his family and friends. On one occasion in 1936, he played the flute with a small string and woodwind ensemble organized for the three-night performance of *Squaring the Circle*, a musical by Valentine Katayev.[17]

Sommerville was less comfortable with his music than he was with painting and acting. He preferred listening to Beethoven, Mozart, and conservative Russian composers. He disliked any form of modern music and virtually nothing outside the classics. As the professor of a course in aesthetics, which he described as an "examination into the qualities causing excellence in the higher arts (architecture, music, poetry, painting and sculpture),"[18] perhaps he felt it was necessary to take the more conservative view. Moreover, Sommerville was more of a devotee of the arts, which is rather different from being a trained expert. As a devotee, he was concerned with the preservation of the "higher arts" as he understood them to be.

Dr. Sommerville held a definite view of what constituted good art. In 1939, while lamenting the changes which were occurring on the international scene since he was a lad, he included a commentary on the arts:

> ...As to the arts, all cannons have been brushed aside as so much rubbish; anything goes now, and the uglier and more bizarre it be, the better is its chance of acclaim. Prose literature plays up vulgarity, obscenity and dirt; poetry descends to formless, unmusical prose; music is converted into noise; sculpture becomes a distorted "What is it?"; prize winning paintings must be absurd in drawing and garish in color. Almost it seems that we have become devotees of the cult of the ugly. It takes some agility to become adapted to it.[19]

Sommerville never had the agility to get used to what he considered to be the new art or new music. According to Mr. Don Evans, Professor-Emeritus of Art, Sommerville was vocal on this point as he refused to work with lines, forms, space, or color in any abstract way, never getting beyond an "academic realism."[20] Although his style had appeal to some and was suited perhaps to the portrait, others did not care for his work. He once complained to his friend and former student, William Shackelford, that some of his teachers and colleagues were merciless in their criticism of his work.

Knowing how he felt about any form of abstraction presented a particular problem to Don Evans when he accepted an offer from the Class of 1933 to paint Dr. Sommerville's portrait. Mr. Evans' style is to be quite interpretative with his subject matter, making use of bright and various colors in relationship to the form for emphasis. His skill with contours and angles, in relationship to the colors tends to place an especial emphasis on the figure itself, and nearly all of his portraits have an abstract quality about them. When he arrived at Dr. Sommerville's home to do the sketches for the portrait he found a formal man in a black formal suit, seated in an arm chair with a bookcase filled with old worn books in the background. He found the entire scene to be "unforgivably drab" but painted it as such because he knew that Sommerville would not like the portrait otherwise. As the work was not his usual kind of painting, Mr. Evans neither signed nor dated the portrait.

A Means of Entertainment

Although Richard Sommerville's leisure time during his youth and in later life was immersed in art, drama, music and reading, his was the last generation before motion pictures and television replaced the necessity for people to create their own forms of entertainment. He was aware of the changing times and often persuaded his friends and colleagues to participate in plays, or discussion groups where newly developing ideas as well as classics were discussed. Although he tended to be very serious he had a lighter side. While he preferred reading the more classical works by writers like Charles Dickens and Shakespeare, on one occasion, he combined his interest in reading, acting, art, and history on canvas by drawing a self-portrait. Giving himself a Dickens "hairdo," he titled it, *Disraeli* after the part he was playing at the time in *Victoria Regina*. He was more amused than serious about this activity, as was his friend, Mr. Shackelford, who now owns the sketch.

Although Sommerville preferred reading the Bible in Greek, he also read Greek and Latin poetry and prose for

Self-Portrait
Sommerville as Disraeli in Victoria Regina
(COURTESY OF MR. W.W. SHACKELFORD)

relaxation. His memory banks included entire poems and memorable lines from poetry and prose in four languages. Known for his tendency to bring forth a poem or nursery rhyme at just the right moment, he especially enjoyed reciting poems to children in his neighborhood, and playing characters like the Pied Piper with them. Often he sketched their portraits as presents to them. From poetry on the sidewalk to children, to the unsettling criticism by noted art critics, to whatever role he assumed on stage, Sommerville was endeavoring to live his definition of the well-rounded life. Without his art, clearly he would have been a very lonely man.

Notes

1. *Charter Members and Minutes and Annual Meetings, November 1921 to May 1949.* Jones Memorial Library. Lynchburg, Virginia.

2. *Little Theatre Scrap Book 1921-29,* Jones Memorial Library.

3. Play Bill, "Meet the Cast," *Little Theatre Scrap Book, 1948-53.* Jones Memorial Library.

4. Robert Hailey. Interview with author. Lynchburg, Virginia, 3 June 1987.

5. Polly Payne. Interview with author. Lynchburg, Virginia, July 1987.

6. Richard Clarke Sommerville, "Faculty Hob-nobs," *The Prism, 1* (January 1939): 5.

7. *Catalogue of Lynchburg College, 1932-33*

8. Ruth Homes Blunt, *The Lynchburg Art Club and Its Affiliates.* (Lynchburg: The Mutual Press.), 40.

9. Ibid., 14.

10. *Annual Report of the Lynchburg Art Club*; *Roster of the Lynchburg Art Club.* Jones Memorial Library, Lynchburg, Virginia.

11. *The Prism,* (May 1946): 5.

12. *Who's Who In American Art,* Alice Coe McGlanflin, ed.

(Washington, D.C.: The American Federation of Art 1936-37), 108.

13. Blunt, 47.

14. *Lynchburg Art Club Scrapbook 1891-1951*

15. *Lynchburg Art Club Scrapbook #1: 1924-59* Other paintings that he is known to have exhibited over the years include: *Quiet War*, date unknown, Lynchburg Art Club; *Portrait* Seventh Annual Exhibition, November 5-20, 1938; *Broom Sage*, Display of First Time Works by League Members, March 30, 1940; *October* and *November*, Lynchburg Art Club Exhibition, April 19, 1945; *Oaks by the Lake*, Lynchburg Art Club, December 1-5, 1946; *Mountains at Elon*, Lynchburg Art Club, October 30 - November 6, 1949; *Lakeside*, Lynchburg Art Club, October 9-15, 1949; *Meadow* and *Young Girl*, May 27, 1950; *Essay in Water Colors*, Georgia Morgan Civic Art Exhibit, September 20, 1954.

16. Blunt, 85.

17. Play Bill, *Squaring the Circle*, 1936.

18. *The Catalogue of Lynchburg College, 1927-28*, 74.

19. See Note 6, p. 7.

20. Don Evans. Interview with author, June 1987.

10

THE EMERITUS YEARS

...“Let me step aside without ceremony.”

R ichard Sommerville formally retired from Lynchburg College at the end of the 1945-46 academic term. He was then seventy years old and had been allowed to remain as the head of the Division of Psychology and Education even after the age of sixty-five. This was unusual even for those days. Typically one could teach until the age of seventy, but administrative positions were not normally maintained after the age of sixty-five. In anticipation of his retirement, in January of 1946, he sought to influence the nature of the recognition that he might receive. He penned his request in a letter to Riley B. Montgomery, president of Lynchburg College, dated January 31, 1946:

My dear President Montgomery,

As the time approaches for me to relinquish my active duties at Lynchburg College, I wish to express to you my thanks for the unfailing consideration and courtesy which you have shown to

173

me as a member of your faculty. I should also like to be permitted to say that I have come to feel a great respect and admiration for your very efficient, intelligent and broad-minded administration of the difficult duties of your office. It has been a privilege to be associated with a man of such calibre.

For myself, I have a request to make. It is that, when the time comes for me to retire from this academic scene, I may be allowed to do so quietly and unobtrusively. Perhaps I assume too much. But the ceremonies observed last year in connection with retirements give me ground to fear their repetition. I should like to be spared such an ordeal.

Specifically, I do not desire a book of letters. The knowledge that they had been solicited would raise the suspicion that some, at least, were written perfunctorily; and that would tend to vitiate all. And as for a dinner with speeches, that is too painfully suggestive of being an auditor at one's own obsequies. I do not feel like being buried yet.

And so, I beg, let me step aside without ceremony.

I am
Respectfully and Sincerely,
Richard Sommerville

On March 1 of that year, he received a letter from President Montgomery which assured him that his wishes would be taken into account, but it said that since he was held in such high esteem by the alumni, the board of trustees, students, and his colleagues, they might want to do something which was appropriate to his years of service to the school.

President Riley Montgomery recommended to the board of trustees that same year that Sommerville be made Professor-Emeritus. The president's citation read:

Lynchburg College loses from its faculty this year by retirement Dr. Richard C. Sommerville who has been for a period of eighteen years one of its most effective and devoted teachers and counselors.
Before coming to Lynchburg College in 1928, Dr.

Sommerville had engaged in educational work as administrator and as teacher. He brought with him in addition to his erudition a rich background of preparation and experience.

As a teacher, Dr. Sommerville inspires his students to creative thought and noble living; as a counselor of young men and women, he wins confidence and devotion; and as a friend, he shares in mutual trust the inner qualities of his refined character and his Christian Spirit.

Among his colleagues he is held in high esteem and respect. The administration depends upon him for wise and sympathetic counsel in matters of educational program and policies.

His versatility, his wide human interests, his keen intellectual ability, and his gentlemanly attitude give him recognition in and entree into the life of the community. He serves faithfully in his church and in various civic and cultural groups. In all his relationships he wins praise for himself and brings honor to Lynchburg College.

In the new position of Professor-Emeritus we shall anticipate having his continued fellowship in the life of the college and in the wider community.[1]

As President Montgomery predicted, the students did honor Dr. Sommerville; they allocated a page of the May 24, 1946 *Critograph* for a citation:

To Dr. Richard Clarke Sommerville, who served so long and faithfully in the halls of Lynchburg College, and is now retiring from his duties, we do dedicate this portion of our paper.

    —To know you is to love you.

    —We considered it a privilege to have had you share your vast store of wisdom and knowledge with us.

    —We regret that others will not have the opportunities to know you and hear you.

    —We hope that the many years yet ahead of you will be filled with the joys and pleasures which you so greatly deserve.

    —We thank you for your patience with us and your wisdom in dealing with our problems.[2]

Likewise his retirement did not go unnoticed by the

editor of the local papers. On June 4, 1946, the following editorial was printed:

AFTER FIFTY YEARS

Thirteen (sic) of the fifty years he has spent in the profession of teaching were spent by Dr. Richard C. Somerville (sic) at Lynchburg College where he was chairman of the division of philosophy and psychology. (sic) During those thirteen years at Lynchburg College Dr. Somerville became an integral part of the intellectual and artistic and social life of Lynchburg. Now that he is retiring his friends in Lynchburg as well as his professional colleagues will hope that he plans to remain with us.

Dr. Sommerville has been actively engaged in the Little Theater, has been a member of discussion groups, has as a painter participated in the activities of Lynchburg's artists and has usually been found in any gathering where matters of more than ordinary interest had drawn people together to enrich the life of the community.

Those groups with which he has associated will look forward to more assurance of his presence with them, to more of his good conversation and discussion, so that his retirement will prove to be a time for more leisure to add to the pleasure of those who always accord him special welcome.

He will teach no less because of his formal retirement. There is too much for him still to impart to all who have the privilege of his company.[3]

With his new title as Professor-Emeritus, Dr. Sommerville did have all rights and privileges of the faculty and access to the campus. Unlike many retirees, he simply kept on with as much of academia as he could. He continued to attend the faculty meetings where he participated in the discussions, voted, made and seconded motions. He continued serving on committees of the faculty, as well as on special committee assignments appointed by the board of trustees. The only difference was that he no longer sat on the executive council of the faculty nor served as the faculty representative to such groups as the Student Government or the Honor Court.

Within SPECS, where he had already served as vice-president five times, as well as recording secretary and president, he again held the office of vice-president for the 1947-48 term. This involvement continued until well into the fifties. When SPECS was disbanded and replaced by an Omega Chapter of Chi Beta Phi, a national scientific fraternity, he was among the first to be tapped into membership in 1954. He continued to give papers at least for two more years. On April 8, 1947 in a paper, "The Mesomorphic Revolution", he clearly demonstrated his continuing interests in physical anthropology and psychology. Using theories developed by W. H. Sheldon of Harvard, claiming that there are basically three predominant body builds which correlate with three predominate personality types, he presented a critical analysis of the cultural, architectural, and dress code changes of his day. Although told whimsically, and more in line with an after dinner speech, his thesis was that the evolved mesomorph (the more robust and muscular body build which Sheldon said was correlated with a more open and active personality), was the underlying influence for functional changes in dress, manners, furniture, and in home architecture.[4]

He was delighted when, despite his retirement, he was called back to teach three courses during the 1947-48 academic term. *The Bulletin of Lynchburg College* (1948-49) announced that a major in psychology would be offered for the first time in the history of the college. Sommerville and a Mrs. Kirkland were listed as the two major professors in the discipline. The stated goal for the major was to provide a program of study for those students desiring to engage in personnel work in business and industry, or to continue studies in clinical psychology, psychiatry, counseling, teaching, and related fields of psychology. The joint

majors with education and philosophy were still offered.
That his spirits were raised somewhat by being
asked to teach is recorded in a letter he sent to Felix Welton
on September 17, 1948:

> I was automatically retired two years ago, due to a fixed age
> limit which the College has adopted. But each year since I have
> been called back into service for a limited amount of work,
> because of the great increase in the number of students. And
> today I got a hint that may happen again this semester. I had set
> myself for an autumn of complete freedom; but on the other hand
> I rather enjoy continuing to do a little teaching. It freshens me up
> to stay in contact with young people; and, besides it is better for
> a man's mental health to have a regular job.[5]

As recounted earlier, he also continued active
participation in the Lynchburg Little Theatre and the
Lynchburg Art Club, serving as president of the latter
group in 1947-48. His activity was noticed by Dr. Fred
Helsabeck, his former student and now his replacement as
head of the Division of Psychology and Education. Dr.
Helsabeck told him in 1946 that he was not worried about
how he would occupy himself in retirement with his many
hobbies and interests in the fine arts. In reply, Dr.
Sommerville said: "Hobbies cease to be hobbies when
they are all that one has to look forward to."[6] At that time
he was unaware of the teaching duties to come, and
without the prospect of the classroom he was quite sad.

"The Incident"

Dr. Sommerville's activity in the life of the campus
and his identity as a professor was so ingrained in him that
when the school again came upon troublesome times, he
put himself in the thick of the events. He became involved

not only because of his identity, but also out of a sense that the college was behaving appropriately. For two years prior to his retirement, Lynchburg College had been selected to participate in one of the projects developed by the Council on Cooperation in Teacher Education, a group formed in Washington, D.C., to study intergroup relations. The aim of this group was to foster interfaith and interracial communications and cooperation. There were many aspects to this study including topics of religious programming to meet the needs of students, race relations, and social cleavages on and off the campus.[7]

Since 1945, Dr. Sommerville had been on the Religious Studies Committee where he remained through 1948.[8] The committee studying race relations had sponsored a number of extended exchange visits between the college and Virginia State University, an all-black college. Some sixty faculty and students had attended the Southern Youth Congress at Columbia, South Carolina. Students were also working at the all-black recreation center in the Lynchburg community. For three years better understanding between the races was encouraged in many ways. Speakers to the campus had included such notables as Sherwood Eddy, Langston Hughes, Ellis Arnold, and Henry Noble MacCracken, and in this segregation era, separate seating was not required at public functions nor were interactions between the students restricted.[9]

At one of the student functions in late February of 1948, there was some socializing and the local students were dancing. A white male asked a black female and they began to dance, but presently the bell signaled time to move to the next function. But the deed of dancing between the races had been done, which did not meet with the approval of some members of the campus or the community. Eventually it got into the newspapers and by March 2, 1948 the headlines read: "President Montgomery Explains

Race Incident." The president explained the purpose of the visits, the greater study and its scope, and he apologized for the "injudicious behavior."

"The incident" was to be a greater concern. There was so much stir about it mainly because the newspaper kept it going. By March 6, 1948, the headlines were saying that a board of trustees meeting would be called to discuss the "race incident." On March 8 at the regular faculty meeting, the faculty were requested to send representatives to a special meeting of the executive committee of the board to be held that night. Following the meeting, the faculty met informally to discuss their positions. They agreed unanimously that this was a small incident, nothing to compare to what the president had accomplished. Some vowed to go with the president if he were forced to resign. They were also unanimous in feeling that they should continue to participate in the intergroup project.[10] As an indication of their resolve they selected from among their membership four of the most respected and beloved members. Dr. Sommerville was asked to attend, but initially declined because of a previous commitment. Later he thought better of it, canceled his plans, and attended the meeting anyway, apparently just walking in. At this meeting, when the faculty were asked to speak, Dr. Sommerville spoke first and emphasized the president's accomplishments. He pointed out that Dr. Montgomery had not been in town during "the incident" and could, therefore, not be held responsible for the actions which had taken place. The others spoke in like manner and clearly stated the views of the faculty.[11]

No resignation was requested but a meeting of the fuller board was called for March 22, 1948 to review the situation. In the meantime, the controversy continued with people writing letters to the editor expressing sentiment in the press.[12] News articles also continued about the executive committee's decision to call a full board meeting.[13] Other events surrounding the issue were also reported.[14]

On March 22, 1948, the trustees did meet to review the situation. Concerns were expressed about sentiments in some quarters of the community which thought that the college was too liberal and revolutionary, as opposed to evolutionary, on social issues. The adverse publicity, resulting from the behavior of some faculty and students which might affect community support for the college's programming, was of concern. In this "era of the Red Scare," some in the community were beginning to suggest that elements of communism were present on the campus! A special committee was appointed to draw up standards for college governance, and another was appointed to study public relations within the community.

The months ahead were not to be peaceful, however, for the faculty or the administration. The college had an extensive lecture series every week at assemblies and on May 4, 1948, Dr. A.J. Muste, the national secretary of the Fellowship of Reconciliation, a national pacifist organization, lectured on world peace on the campus. This was his second visit.[15] However, this visit enraged the editor of the local newspaper and editorials appeared in both *The News* and *The Daily Advance*, May 5 and May 6, 1948. In the latter, an editorial titled, "Enough is Enough," appeared and aside from reacting to the statements by Mr. Muste, the editor accused the school of bringing in too many pacifists as Muste had appeared there before and that a Japanese-American pacifist had also appeared there once.[16] The editorial intoned:

...The College has had speakers of this stripe enough to prove its 'liberalism'. It might be the part of wisdom to neglect them for a while now, lest people get the idea that the college authorities are in the conspiracy against world peace in which wittingly or unwittingly, and not all are simpletons—these people are engaged. Especially is this true when there is is (sic) not even the excuse of bringing to the college campus men of importance, or notoriety if not of fame, but emphasis is upon men who are hardly known outside a few sinister or naive groups.

For some reason the editor did not mention the fact that Norman Thomas, who ran for President of the United States in 1928 and 1932 on the Socialist party ticket, debated the noted journalist J.T. Graves of Birmingham, Alabama, on the issue of universal military training on the campus on February 16, 1948.[17] Additionally, the Minnesota congressman, Walter Judd, who strongly supported universal military training, had spoken at the assembly exercises the week prior to Muste's second appearance, as had other local citizens. The editorial said that although not all students were influenced by these talks, some were "impressed" and their parents ought to keep these students at home to shield them from such influence.

Again on May 6, 1948, in *The Daily Advance*, a more serious editorial appeared. Titled simply, "Lynchburg College," it said that within the community, that part who are friends of the college are upset over the series of programs and incidents on the campus which have gone on for years. It also claimed that the programming was against the American welfare and implied that "communist influences at work" on the campus were helping to contribute to communist ideology. It went on to say that if such is true, then the college, dependent upon the community for funds as well as for students, was not only hurting itself, but also "the interests of that college's graduates when they look for a job..."

This particular editorial so upset the Chairman of the Board of Trustees, Dr. John Tate, that he called the

Richmond office of the Federal Bureau of Investigation and asked for a full-scale investigation. He further wrote a letter to *The News* stating his actions, and saying that he did not believe any of it. He simply wanted the college's name cleared.[18] The paper not only printed the letter, but also ran headlines: "FBI Asked to Probe Red Influence at LC."

In response to the accusations, the faculty met unofficially on May 10, 1948 and drafted a response to the editorial. The letter, along with an introductory news report was published on Wednesday, May 12, 1948. The faculty stated that college students are not children and are not in need of protection from differing viewpoints. The balanced presentation of the points of view were chronicled. They asked to be allowed to teach in an atmosphere of open and free inquiry, without fear of reprisals. They asserted their abhorrence of communism and their respect for democracy. Richard Sommerville's signature was the first on the letter which was accompanied by thirty-six members of the faculty.

In the same edition of *The News* in which the letter from the faculty was printed another editorial appeared claiming to have been misunderstood and called the faculty "careless readers." The editor accused them of many mistaken ideas and said that they had missed his point.

That point was not that Dr. A.J. Muste, a cracked-brain advocate of cracked-brain theories, spoke at the college, or that any particular advocate of any particular cause has spoken. The point was not that students might be influenced by the pacifists and extreme radicals who have spoken, for the belief was plainly expressed that the students, though immature, would not be impressed by the manifest absurdities these speakers have pouted. The point is, as expressed in the headline, Enough is Enough, and in the body of last Thursday's editorial was that no balance is maintained, that programs are so weighted to one side so as to suggest purpose. In other words the dictum that all sides must be heard is not relevant when the complaint is that one side is being heard more than the others.[19]

Over the next several weeks, in support of the school, two students also responded to the editorial and to others who had complained about the school.[20]

The college was to stay in the media. But this series of newspaper-Lynchburg College debates were not new to the college nor to the town. From September 25, 1947 through May 11, 1948, President Riley Montgomery, who was an executive officer of the Federal Council of Churches and president of the Virginia Council of Churches, had publicly defended that organization against charges from the many factions which saw it as a liberal organization. In September of 1947, a group of Presbyterian ministers and laymen from around the South and Southeast met in Lynchburg to discuss their withdrawal from that organization. Their concerns were similar to those expressed by segments of other religious denominations. They thought that the Federal Council of Churches advocated pacifist positions, non-segregation of the races, abolition of the free enterprize system, socialized medicine, and had too broad a theological platform.[21] Additionally, President Montgomery had taken a strong personal and public stand against universal military training, whereas the paper, reflecting popular sentiment in Lynchburg at least, strongly supported it.[22] All of these issues were hotly debated as 1948 was a national election year. All of the national candidates addressed many of these issues in their platforms. Local candidates in Lynchburg thought the town had its own examples to address.

The annual board of trustees meeting was coming on June 3, 1948, and of their own volition, students got a petition up in support of the president.[23] Likewise the

Alumni Association called for support of the president.[24] Ministers and laymen of the Disciples Churches of the Chesapeake Area also stood behind the college.[25]

At the board meeting, a committee composed of faculty and trustees submitted a statement of policies for administration of the college. Richard Sommerville, the three others who had represented the faculty before, and two other members had been appointed to work on the resolution.[26] The resolution was passed unanimously and was reprinted in its entirety in *The News*, June 4, 1948. The next day an editorial of support of the college appeared in *The News*.

The possibility that Dr. Montgomery might resign regardless of the widespread support exhibited, occurred to Dr. Tate. He and a few members of the executive committee had discussed the idea of asking Dr. Richard Clarke Sommerville to become acting-president until a successor could be named.[27]

Whether or not Dr. Sommerville knew this, given his personality, he would have accepted. Moreover, at least in terms of the global debatable issues, the college programming probably would not have changed. Sommerville had found nothing on the campus to be one-sided or biased despite the fact that he had declared himself not to be a pacifist, and like the editor, blamed pacifists in part for Hitler's fearless rise to power. He wholeheartedly supported not only universal military training, but a world government, one which would be outspoken against communism. He was even more vocal on the need for a free and an open discussion of all and any debatable points of view. While he could have easily stayed away from the controversy, he chose not to. Non-involvement would clearly have meant abrogating his duty, not only to the president whom he respected and with whom he did not always agree, but to the school. He would have failed to stand up for his beliefs on free inquiry and free speech. "I believe in the high value of human liberty and am thankful that I live in a country where it is still possible for a man to stand up in public and, with due regard for dissenting opinion and the common good, say what he honestly thinks. Priceless liberty; may we guard it well!"

In 1949, Riley Montgomery did, in fact, resign after receiving an invitation to become president of the College of the Bible in Lexington, Kentucky. He was inaugurated on September 27, 1949 and Richard Sommerville represented the president of Lynchburg College, Dr. Orville Wake, as his official delegate.[29]

The Student's Plea

After the three years of excitement, Sommerville settled into a new routine. His former students were now his friends. Enjoying good health, he tended his formal garden and fruit trees, the produce from which he enjoyed sharing with his friends. He painted daily in the studio that he had set up in his home, exhibited his works and continued participating in plays for various groups. However, the thing he most enjoyed and still wanted was the classroom.

In the fall of 1950, he apparently did not have a class to teach, which made him very unhappy. He wrote a letter to one of his favorite students, Stuart Bruchey, who in turn wrote the following:

January 2, 1950

Dear Dr. Wake,

It is with mixed feelings of presumption, guilt and deep sympathy that I enclose a letter I recently received (the letter was not preserved) from Dr. Richard Sommerville. I feel certain you will not disclose to him my action and that the subject will remain one of high confidence between us.

Although I am not personally known to you as a former student at Lynchburg College (1937-39) I recollect with warmth and devotion the ineffaceable respect for humanity which my every experience at the school inculcated in me. Employed now as a Department of the Army historian and also completing work for my PhD at Johns Hopkins, I feel particularly indebted to Dr. Sommerville for his role in laying the Christian foundation for my continuing education. Our relationship comprised more than an elemental one between teacher and student. He was the beloved master, and I the devoted apprentice. I remember hours at his feet, seated on the grass in his garden. I remember the substance of long, cherished walks together in the hills. We have corresponded for more than ten years. For many years after leaving Lynchburg I got back at least once a year to see him.

The thought that he is no longer teaching because, I presume, of his age, fills me with a pain of regret, not only for his sake but also for the young lives he might otherwise indelibly impress in the way he did mine. Is it not possible, by some wise modification of tradition and rule, to invite him to teach one course a year, in General Psychology or in the Introduction to Philosophy? It is not only because older men frequently die not long after the removal of the busy centers of their lives. It is primarily because he has so much to give. Years of thoughtful living have seasoned his knowledge with wisdom. I think of the incalculable loss the nation would suffer if men like Bernard Baruch or Herbert Hoover were debarred by age from enriching the national life by the irreplaceable contributions of their distilled experiences. Are not elder statesmen and elder teachers in a very important sense irreplaceable? If you find that Dr. Sommerville is not feeble or incapacitated I deeply hope you will be able to permit him to give to the life of the College what, so uniquely, he has to contribute.

Sincerely,
Stuart Bruchey

On January 12, 1950, President Wake responded by expressing his appreciation for Mr. Bruchey's thoughtfulness and expressed that, during his student days, Sommerville had the same appeal to him. "I have the greatest admiration and respect for him as a person and a teacher. There are many alumni who inquire about him as I go from place to place in the interest of the College." He explained that while Dr. Sommerville was not actively teaching, he was participating in the occasional faculty meeting, and he had been frequently asked to represent the college in an official capacity. He closed with assurances that "We shall continue to do all that we can to preserve his magnificent influence here on the campus and in the life of the College."

The following term, Dr. Sommerville taught evening classes in philosophy. Upon learning that he was to teach again, his former student, Stanley Jordan returned to take the course from him once again. Sommerville was called back every session to teach at least one course and sometimes two until the age of 79 when his services were no longer required. During those years, he continued to teach in the same style as he had in previous years, but now many of the mannerisms that had once been viewed by students as deliberate and considered were now sometimes seen as eccentricities of age. However, he was still recognized for his friendly disposition toward others and many, like his former students of earlier years, were impressed by his store and range of knowledge.

In 1953, he also returned to the Lynchburg College stage where he played Polonious in *Hamlet*. After this performance, members of the Epsilon Chapter of *Alpha Psi Omega*, a national honorary dramatic fraternity, made him an honorary member. Student reporter, Yon Schoenmaker, who met him during the performances, interviewed him in his home for yet another feature article of his life, bringing the total number of such interviews to at least six since 1928.[30]

At some point, he began to write essays on the history of philosophy and the history of science. When he died, his personal papers along with his books, journals, diaries, and dissertation material, were all donated to Lynchburg College. However, repeated searches on the part of many persons have failed to locate these materials. His books were not kept as a private collection nor were records kept of his holdings. In the mid-sixties, the name plates were removed from all of the books as part of a reclassification system. The only remaining identifiable paper is on Syngman Rhee's ancestry, rise to power, and the beginning years of his rule as president of South Korea. The paper is undated, but references up through 1956 are included. At some point he either gave a talk or was planning to give one, probably to the Club 13, because there is also an envelope with abbreviated notes inside.

He continued to be remembered, however, in other ways. In 1957, the board of trustees awarded him an Honorary Doctor of Laws degree during the commencement exercises when he was recognized not only for outstanding service to the school, but also for outstanding service to the community art programs and humanity in general. The citation on this occasion was primarily a brief life review and included the following:

> In Professor Sommerville's classes, generations of students had the exhilarating experience of knowing vividly the broad sweep of human culture. His colleagues on the faculty and his friends in the community felt themselves enriched by contact with one who in his mind and spirit exemplified classical balance and control, and in the best sense of the term, true humanism.

The Most Personal Challenge

On October 19, 1959, one week after his eighty-fourth birthday, while returning from a dinner invitation at the home of Miss Nancy Mattox, a former student and personal friend, he was struck by a car. The vehicle, driven by a twenty-year-old college student, hit him at the corner of Vernon Street and Langhorne Lane near Wingfield Street. He was dragged over twenty feet, and then thrown another twenty-four feet, according to newspaper accounts.[31] He suffered severe bilateral contusions of both legs, a cracked pelvis, contusions, and other lacerations about the face and body. Miraculously, although he had a slight concussion, he escaped severe head injuries. His condition was critical for weeks, and ultimately, it was complicated by pneumonia. If he would ever walk again was seriously questioned. According to Dr. Robert Brickhouse, his attending physician, the concern was over his age and the severity of the broken legs. However, Sommerville was determined to get on his feet. After spending more than nine months in the hospital and another three months recovering in the home of George and Melva Adams, he was able to walk again with the aid of crutches, and later with the use of one cane.

His recovery was not without problems, yet eager to recover, he decided to dictate both the time table of his recovery and the nature of his hospital care. This put him at odds with his physician, Dr. Brickhouse. He felt that Sommerville was not recovering as quickly as he otherwise could because he had become too reliant on the three private duty nurses who attended him around the clock. He advocated reducing the number of nurses and sending Dr. Sommerville to a convalescent home. Apparently interpreting this as a signal that he would never walk again, and dreading the idea of a nursing home, Dr. Sommerville sent word to Dr. Brickhouse that his services were no longer needed. He asked for another physician. According to Dr. Brickhouse, this was arranged to everyone's satisfaction and Dr. Sommerville kept his nurses and his hospital room.[32]

During his recovery both in the hospital and later in the Adams home, he continued to write essays on the history of science, and was also busy responding to the many cards and letters that he was receiving from his friends and acquaintances. From time to time his condition was reported in the local papers. Long before he was discharged from the hospital, he was allowed to go for an afternoon drive with friends.

The Final Tribute in Life

In 1960, members of the class of 1933, for whom Dr. Sommerville had been the class sponsor, decided to honor him again. Spearheaded by the efforts of Dr. Meredith Norment, Jr., president of the class and director of College Relations, a portrait was commissioned which was to become part of the college's permanent collection. The painting was to be hung in Hopwood Hall, the building in which Dr. Sommerville taught all his classes. As indicated earlier, Professor Don Evans, then chairman of the Department of Art, was commissioned to do the work. Ceremonies marking the unveiling were held in conjunction with Homecoming Weekend on September 21, 1960. Citations from those ceremonies are as follows:

A Citation

As a teacher Dr. Richard Clarke Sommerville had the ability to make vivid for his students the great achievements of mankind. He could range freely over the history of culture, drawing illustrations from the arts and the sciences. He brought to his classes a rich background of training and a continuing interest in the classics; in music, painting, drama, and literature; in philosophy, psychology, and education. Always he had a

Portrait of Richard Sommerville
W. Donald Evans, Artist
Commissioned by the Class of 1933
(COURTESY OF LYNCHBURG COLLEGE ART COLLECTION —
VIRGINIA DAVIS, CURATOR)

genius for causing the individual student to feel that the student's experience in learning, and the student's philosophy was life, were of genuine importance.

With dignity, versatility, ability, and devotion, he has moved among us for a long period of years. Young people feel themselves nobler for having been in his presence. For generations of Lynchburg College students he has come to be a symbol of the gifted teacher, the humane scholar, the accomplished gentleman. The portrait which we unveil today will remind us always of his great spirit and his vital influence.

John M. Turner, Jr.
Dean of the College, 1952-1972

An Appreciation

Deliberate in his speech as in his daily life, Richard Clarke Sommerville displayed the qualities he instructed his students to emulate: patience, courage, dedication.

Dr. Sommerville was a man of profound thought and able scholarship, as well as of Christian culture. Dr. M.E. Sadler, former Lynchburg College Dean and now Chancellor of Texas Christian University, once said of him, "Dr. Sommerville is the most fully, beautifully educated man I ever knew."

A man of letters with up-to-date knowledge of scientific advance, his benign, strong countenance bespoke a deep understanding of persons and of human relationships, and revealed both his articulate wisdom and quiet courage.

A man of remarkable versatility, he was an artist, musician, actor, and ardent churchman. In the community of both college and city, exhibiting a keen interest in all these phases of his well-rounded life, this gentleman-scholar evoked wide-spread admiration and deep respect.

As philosopher, Dr. Sommerville was indeed a true lover of truth; as teacher, he ably communicated what he knew; as friend, he was ever faithful. Above all, and with all his wisdom and several abilities, he was an humble and upright child of God, in whom he *really* lived and moved and had his being.

Rev. W. Meredith Norment, Jr.

Dr. Sommerville is a man I have esteemed for 12 years, so
when the alumni asked me some two years ago to undertake the
painting, I saw it as a projection of their wish for a tribute to a
well-loved teacher, mentor, a distinguished man of learning.
During the sessions of work at Dr. Sommerville's home and at
mine, I learned further that his is a quality of mind and spirit
which in its radiation becomes the more cogent; or as a poet has
the better said it, "an instance of goodness diffused, and in the
diffusion made more intense."

W. Don Evans

Dr. Sommerville was able to attend all the functions associated with the unveiling. He appeared remarkably well despite his handicaps. He recovered and resumed
work in his garden and moved about the community when
accompanied by others. He was now more willing to call
on others for attention, such as his friend, Lavelon Sydnor.
He would confess that "the lonesomeness is getting to
me." Mr. Sydnor would pick him up and take him to his
home, usually for dinner and always for a game of Scrabble.
These occasions always called for a cigar and an ice cream
cone, two "privileges" that Sommerville never relinquished.

In November of 1962, Dr. Sommerville was felled
by a stroke. This was to be his final challenge in life. He
spent his final days at St. John's Nursing Home, where
both the nurses and his friends sensed that Sommerville
knew the end was near.[33] He died on February 23, 1963. At
his request, his body was sent home to White Post, Virginia,
to be buried alongside his parents in the family plot in
Mount Hebron Cemetery near Winchester, in the place
that he had called home all his life.

Notes

1. *Minutes of the Board of Trustees*, June 3, 1946.
2. *The Critograph*, 32, 15 (May 24, 1946): 4.

3. *The News* (June 4, 1946), 2.

4. Richard Clarke Sommerville, "The Mesomorphic Revolution," *Minutes of the SPECS Club*, April 8, 1947.

5. Letter from Richard Sommerville to Felix and Francis Welton, 17 September 1948. Welton Family Papers.

6. Fred Helsabeck, Interview with author, 16 April 1983.

7. L. A. Cook, ed., *Intergroup Relations in Teacher Education. I* (Washington, D.C. American Council on Education 1950-51), 246.

8. *Minutes Faculty Council*, October 29, 1947.

9. Fred Helsabeck and Weldon Thompson, "Intergroup Relations at Lynchburg College," In Cook, (1950-51), 245-269.

10. *Minutes of the Faculty* March 8, 1948.

11. *Minutes of the Executive Committee*, March 8, 1948.

12. *The News*, March 21, 1948 carried five letters.

13. *The Daily Advance*, March 9, 1948; *The News*, March 10, 1948. In Riley Montgomery, *Reminiscences of Riley Benjamin Montgomery, I, II,* (Unpublished Autobiography, Lynchburg College Archives).

14. *The News*, March 9, 1948. In Montgomery, 1974.

15. His first was during World War II in February, 1944.

16. He did in March, 1944.

17. *The Critograph, 24*, 8 (Thursday, February 19, 1948): 1

18. *The News,* May 11, 1948. In Montgomery, 1974.

19. Ibid., May 12, 1948.

20. Ibid., May 16, 1948; May 9, 1948.

21. See *The News*, September 27, 1947.

22. See the Editorial, *The News*, February 22, 1948.

23. *The Daily Advance*, May 20, 1948.

24. *The Daily Advance*, May 26, 1948.

25. *The Daily Advance,* June 1, 1948; *Reminiscences of Riley Montgomery*, 1974.

26. Letter, Riley Montgomery to Richard Sommerville, 2 April 1948.

27. Presidential Papers of Riley Montgomery, File 2/8/6, Box 7, Lynchburg College Archives.

28. Richard Clarke Sommerville, "As a Man Thinketh," *The Prism, 2* (February, 1940): 16.

29. Letter, Orville Wake to Richard Sommerville, 13

September 1949.

30. *The Critograph,* (March 13, 1953): 5.

31. *The News,* October 20, 1959.

32. Dr. Robert Brickhouse, interview by phone with author, 10 June 1987.

33. Fred Helsabeck, Interview with author, 16 April 1983.

EPILOGUE

U pon his death, a few members of the faculty met informally to discuss establishing a special scholarship in memory of Richard Clarke Sommerville. A larger group of faculty met on March 20, 1963 to hear proposals and to appoint a special committee charged with formulating the conditions under which the scholarship would be developed and administered. Under the chairmanship of Ruskin S. Freer, the committee consisting of Professors Ruth Bahous, Jeter Parker, W.W. Ferguson, John G. Mahan, Shirley E. Rosser, and M. Weldon Thompson, made the following recommendations:

1. That the faculty of Lynchburg College sponsor the establishment of the scholarship.
2. That a principal sum of $15,000 be raised.
3. That the award to given to the rising senior based on his or her previous three year record at Lynchburg College.
4. That the student receiving the award be designated as *The Sommerville Scholar*.
5. That the qualifications considered be scholarship and character and that neither need, extra-curricular activities, nor other awards be regarded.

197

Moreover, members of the committee felt that the student's *character* should include his or her attitude toward Lynchburg College and the scholarly life generally, as expressed in the phrase so often quoted by Dr. Sommerville, "The scholarly habit and appetite which lead to ever-increasing knowledge."

The committee's recommendations were accepted and a thirty-member committee consisting of faculty and staff along with citizens of the community, alumni, and friends of Dr. Sommerville's, was appointed to spearhead the fund-raising efforts. The first award, given in 1965-66 to Madeline Ann Cyrus, has been given annually to the present time. This award, more than any other accolade given to Richard Sommerville in his lifetime, essentially guaranteed his legacy.

Throughout his life, Richard Sommerville admired the masters of the great disciplines. Able to absorb all that he read, his command of the curriculum awed and inspired others. At the same time, he remained a very practical man with the special talent to communicate across the generations. Richard Sommerville was recognized for excellence in his teaching career and for his social adroitness. In life he was respected and loved by many, but in death, although members of the scholarship committee worked to preserve his memory accurately, his reputation grew. In some respects his reputation turned into a legend of derring-do that really was not true, as in chasing "Pancho" Villa over Texas, or going on posses, or chasing Indians. Perhaps these stories reveal more about modern society's values than about him.

From his years at Hampden-Sydney and throughout his life, clearly he placed great store on "doing one's duty" and admired those who did, especially if their deeds were noble. His peregrinations until after the age of fifty suggest that he was in search of something, for he was unwilling to establish either roots or ties. Although he had held positions of respect in those years, something was missing for him. By sharp contrast, the professor settled in Lynchburg easily. Even following retirement, when his family wanted him nearer, he chose to stay. One can only surmise that Lynchburg College and the community gave him a forum for his many talents. There he was the philosopher-psychologist on the campus, the artist and actor within the fine arts community. There he could and did "speak his peace without fear of reprisal." For him, Lynchburg was not an escape, but the place where he chose to live his definition of the good life. There he was able to live out the remainder of his life unfettered, free, and accepted.

This story has been told, not because he was a hero, not because I wanted to build a monument to him, for that existed long before I ever heard of him. Rather, I went in search of a man of mystery and found a true educator—a lifelong student who studied because he wanted to know. Although Richard Sommerville was a retiring man who could be both formal and dispassionate, he was passionate in his views on the value of education. He believed strongly that the purpose of education was to help the student to develop personal competency, a sense of re-sponsibility, and the ability to make wise, educated choices in life. Further, education should help the students to discover themselves, to seek happiness, and to "take pride in the doing," as he was fond of saying. He always believed that happiness must come from within and can only be understood when one accepts oneself. "Blow your little tin whistles!" This was his message to his students and they remember and appreciate him for it.

APPENDIX A.
Richard Sommerville's Student Writings
Annotated by Elza C. Tiner

These essays were all written while Richard Sommerville
was a student at Hampden-Sydney. Background to these papers,
reprinted from The Hampden-Sidney Magazine, is discussed at
greater length in Chapter 2, section "The Student Writer."

Unlike most of his fellow students who published their work
in the literary magazine, Richard displays an unusual ability to relate
his ideas to other literature. "Oola-Ita," as discussed in Chapter 2, is
a retelling and elaboration of a Dakota legend. In "Some Remarks on
Hand-Shaking," a satiric profile of a human gesture, he refers to
classical and contemporary literary authors who not only mention the
topic, but also are masters of irony, including Horace, Shakespeare,
Dickens, and Sir Herbert Maxwell. "A Slave-Hero," based on personal observation, links a slave's effort to rescue passengers on a
canal boat with the theme of heroism in a variety of genres: poetry,
prose, and drama. Here Richard reveals his broad reading habits and
interest in a wide range of literature.

Oola-Ita

The Hampden-Sidney Magazine 11, 6 (March 1894): 310-314

About forty miles below St. Paul, the Mississippi broadens
out into a long narrow lake, some twenty-five miles in length and
between two and four miles broad. This is Lake Pepin, which, though
perhaps not so well known as some other bodies of water in the United
States, is certainly not lacking in beauty and picturesqueness. In shape
it resembles a great crescent, with its horns turned to the southwest.
On the east shore is a lofty range of lime-stone bluffs, much broken
and crumbled, frequently presenting prospects of the utmost sublim-
ity. On the west, the shore recedes abruptly for a short distance, and
then runs back in a high level prairie, here and there broken by conical
hills, the remains, doubtless, of some ancient tribe of Mound Build-
ers. To-day a railroad runs along this high plateau to the west, and as
one sits at his car window and looks out across the expanse of water
and watches the line of hills on the eastern shore, now clear and

distant, now further removed, here jutting out in a bold promontory and the next moment rapidly receding in the graceful curve of some bay, he will probably see many a rugged precipice which, if he be of a romantic turn of mind, he may easily turn into a typical Lover's Leap; but let him wait until he nears the northern end and then he will see where the eastern shore, as if impatient for its meeting with the western, though already gradually approaching it, suddenly juts out in a bold point, which is in turn abruptly broken off at its extremity, forming a high dangerous precipice. Let him mark it well, for there is a story connected with it—a story as pathetic and as beautiful as any ever told of the heroes of old.

Many years ago—how many I couldn't say, for this story was old when men now gray were still in their prime—there stood near the northern end of Lake Pepin an Indian village in which dwelt a tribe of the Sioux. Now of all the maidens in this village, by far the prettiest, most accomplished and most virtuous was Oola-Ita, the daughter of the brave old chief. None made moccasins so pretty as hers, none so skillful with paint and brush, to decorate the warriors, none so industrious, and none so modest withal, as Oola-Ita.

But Oola-Ita was not yet married. Offers enough had been made for her—offers from old chieftains and young chieftains, chieftains from her own tribe and chieftains from other tribes—offers of fifty ponies, a hundred ponies, bear skins, deer skins, even seal skins, many and few—and still Oola-Ita was unmarried; not for want of offers, not for want of suitors, but because her father had not yet found a combination of offer and suitor which pleased him.

But not because Oola-Ita had not found such a combination; about the offer she with reason gave herself little concern, for she, poor child, would receive none of it, whether it be great or small; but about the suitor she did care, as was quite natural. Among the youngest of the chieftains who gathered round her father's council fire, was Chiska, a young warrior of great bravery and an acknowledged leader among the young men. This chieftain had become much attached to Oola-Ita, who returned his affection, and often would they be together in the forest, he playing the chotunkah, or Indian flute, and she making moccasins and ornaments of beads. But Oola-Ita's father wished that when his daughter married her husband should be a chief of greater power than Chiska, and so he opposed the match.

Now there was a certain old chief, renowned for his wisdom and influence in the nation, who was just the man to suit the maiden's father, and who at last took a fancy to her and sent in a large offer, which was at once accepted by her parents, to her great sorrow and disappointment. In vain did she plead with the father and in vain did Chiska increase his offer to much more than that of his rival; Indian fathers, when making matches, are, as a rule, more attentive to their own interests than to the wishes of the child, and so in this case, the interests of her father demanding her marriage with the more influential chieftain, Oola-Ita had to give up Chiska and prepare to become the bride of his rival.

*   *   *   *   *   *   *   *

And so the days go by until at last it is the evening of the marriage. Indian marriages ordinarily are very simple and require little preparation, but Oola-Ita is the chief's daughter and so her wedding must be as imposing as possible. All day her father's lodge has been a bustle, nor is it quiet yet. Oola-Ita, making no objection, yet evincing no interest, has suffered her mother to array her in all of her savage finery—gay-colored blankets and furs, belts and necklaces and bracelets of wampum, earrings, feathers and what not; and now she sits, ready, waiting. Outside the lodge is bustle and noise and commotion—she heeds it not, for in her breast is a greater conflict and commotion; around her friends and visitors are laughing and talking, but no responsive smile lights the countenance of Oola-Ita; once they called her "Laughing Eyes," but there is no laughter in those eyes now; her thoughts are far away from her present surroundings—the noise and confusion, the lights, the voices, the faces coming and going—far from these things she wanders in her fancy; again she stands under the shade of the forest, in the cool air of the evening; again the birds sing over her head, the flowers bloom under her feet, the warm winds fan her brow; again the plaintive notes of the flute fall on her ear, again she hears a familiar foot-step, and her love is by her side; once more she hears his soft voice as he tells her of the sunny fields of the Southland, the brooks and the meadows, the forest filled with game, with birds above and flowers beneath, the land of the unending summer; again he is telling her how he has been saving up the ponies and wampum, with which to pay her father, that then they might go and dwell in the forest; once more she hears him asking her will she go with him, and again she answers, "yes." And now the scene changes; the events of the last few weeks pass through her mind in quick succession—her father's refusal of Chiska's offer, his acceptance of the old chief's, her ineffectual prayers and entreaties, her days of silent disappointment, her fits of despair, her misgivings at breaking her vow to Chiska, and finally, her plan to avoid breaking that vow. Here her thoughts stop; her heart still recoils from the contemplation of such a terrible deed, yet the more she considers it, the more necessary it seems and the more firm becomes her resolve, until finally her mind is settled, the question is decided. Yes, she will do it. There is no laughter in Oola-Ita's eyes now.

Stealthily she leaves her father's house, passes through the village and on to the hills and the cliffs of the lake beyond. Presently she stands at the extremity of a small point that, suddenly jutting out into the water, ends abruptly in a high precipice. Here she pauses and looks about her. How beautiful and calm is the evening! Over to the left, from behind the dark and irregular range of limestone bluffs along the eastern shore, the moon is just rising, bathing the tops of the rocks in a silvery flood of light; out in the western sky, just above one of those ancient mounds, the evening star gleams brightly, more brilliant, if not so luminous, as its rival in the east; far below and off to the right, lies the village, with its lights and weird figures moving about the camp fires; while in the midst of all, as a gem in its setting, lies the lake, smooth, unruffled, reflecting the stars and the moonlight. No sound disturbs the stillness, save the occasional hoot of an owl or cry of some wild beast in the forest, or when at times a slight breeze bears to the ear subdued murmurs from the village down below; but for these, and the dreaming, monotonous droning of the thousand and one insects of the night, all is silent. Peace is upon the land.

Long and silently Oola-Ita stands and gazes upon this tranquil scene; long and lovingly do her eyes rest upon her native village, upon the hills and the lake and all the familiar objects; rapidly she thinks and wonders—thinks of the past and wonders of the future; once or twice, as she looks at the lake, she shudders and clasps her hands; otherwise, she remains absorbed in thought and motionless.

But her revere is quickly broken; she starts, and listens

intently. Yes, surely she is not mistaken—Some one is coming up the rocks. They have discovered her absence and tracked her. If she delays, they will secure her and her design be frustrated. No time is to be lost. In moment she is at the edge of the precipice; as she glances down at the lake below, so cold, so glassy, so still, a slight tremor passes her frame; but she turns away her eyes and thinks again— "What was it the Sachem said about the Happy Hunting Ground? Would Chiska be there? Would the great spirit be pleased that she kept her vow?" But quick, she must hurry, they are upon her—for a moment her arms are out-stretched towards heaven, her lips move slightly and then—

Oola-Ita's father, coming, at the head of the pursuers, around a boulder at the rear of the precipice, burst upon a spectacle that well-nigh freezes his blood—there in the clear moon-light outlined against the western sky, he beholds the form of his daughter poise for an instant on the brink, and then disappear beyond! Springing forward he is just in time to hear a light splash in the water below, and looking over, sees a great ripple form at the base of the cliff and go spreading out over the waters of the lake; and as it breaks on the opposite shore, the ripple of human life breaks on the shore of Eternity!

Such is the story of Oola-Ita, the untutored Indian maiden, who was ready to sacrifice her life in preference to breaking a sacred vow of betrothal. Let her heroic action, and the nobleness of the mind that prompted it, redeem her name from oblivion.

Some Remarks on Hand-Shaking
The Hampden-Sidney Magazine 12, 1 (October 1894): 15-20.

To-day is peculiarly the day of science; there is a science for moving, eating, sleeping, and even murder has been reduced to a fine art. It is a day of scientific research and investigation, and a subject brought before the public in any other than a scientific manner has, as a rule, small chance of a favorable reception. In view of these facts it is a source of much regret that the scientific method cannot be used in the treatment of the subject in hand; but as a matter of fact, it would hardly be appropriate; there isn't much science about hand-shaking; some persons, it is true, have gotten it down to a science, but the general run of men shake hands pretty much as they please, without regard to any rules or regulations. So the scientific method won't do; we'll just have to roll up our sleeves and, like the old lady in the story, having

* * "Bid farewell to every fear,
  And boldly waded in,"[1]

do our best in our unscientific way, and then when the task is done, have a good hand-shake all around, and end the scene with a toast to the custom.

Before going farther, perhaps it would be interesting to ask ourselves why we should shake each other's hands when we meet rather than do something else, as for instance, pull ears or rub noses or wink eyes or some equally foolish thing. What's the difference? When we read in our geographies that the Malays or Hindoos or Abyssinians or some such barbarous people rub their noses together or fall on the ground when they greet one another, we exclaimed "Oh, how funny!" and thought it very ridiculous indeed. Well, well, *De gustibus*!. I presume the savage would be as much amused by our hand-shaking as we by his nose-rubbing. With all our modern civilization and refinement, we may well ask in what way our manner of greeting is superior to his. For both are only relicts of a remote age of barbarism. You may open your eyes if you will, but it is true nevertheless. Of all the many theories in regard to the origin of the custom of hand-shaking, beyond doubt the most plausible is the one carrying us back to the remotest of savage times, when two men meeting gave each other their weapon hands as a security against treachery or sudden attack. A noble origin, truly! Let us pride ourselves on a custom that commemorates our pristine uprightness and honor!

There are in general two great classes—persons with whom you like to shake hands and persons with whom you dislike to shake hands. It will be convenient here to treat of the last class first, as it is the more formidable one, and the sooner off hand the better.

At the top of the list stands your muscular friend from the country, six feet six, with sinews of iron and a grip like a vice. Ow the memory of it! In his interesting article on *Bores*, Sir Herbert Maxwell conjectures that the accidents in which people are run over and killed in Piccadilly are chiefly owing to two causes—drink and the precipitate flight on the approach of a jocular bore.[2] Now it is true that the majority of jocular bores are disagreeable hand-shakers, but not all disagreeable hand-shakers are jocular bores; so if Sir Herbert had assigned three chief causes—drink, precipitate flight on the approach of a bore and also on the approach of a hand-crushing friend—probably he would have been nearer right.

This is one of the most vicious classes of the whole species. They know their power of inflicting torture and they take a fiendish delight in exercising it upon every one with whom they meet, whether he be great or small, friend or mere acquaintance; they are no respecters of persons. And what adds bitterness to the physical suffering they inflict is the extreme suavity of their manner, the winning cheerfulness of countenance and utmost unconcern with which they always do their cruel work. (sic) Why, hullo, Jones old man!" your tormentor exclaims, swooping upon you at an unexpected moment, "How are you this morning. Why, I haven't seen you for an age! Give me your hand, old boy." He doesn't wait for it to be proffered, but with a skillful movement he seizes it, and then—shades of the fathers preserve us!—the torment begins. Still looking down upon you with the benignest of smiling countenances, he gives one good squeeze—the bones crackle and grate—and then he lets it fall, a crushed, bloodless and aching piece of bone and flesh. And yet you try to laugh and look pleasant when all the while it is only by an effort that you restrain your tears. This is indeed a dreadful man. No wonder persons get run over in Piccadilly in trying to avoid him; his tender mercies are cruel.

And then those long-winded persons—the family minister, the dear old grand-dame who knows by heart all the marriages and deaths and interminglings of your family and every other family, and who always persist in reciting these facts in detail whenever she meets you, and that other old person, the friend of the family who knew "your par and mar when they were little bits of things, no more'n so high" (indicating with his hand), and who takes great delight in pouring into your weary ears a long string of his boyhood reminiscences, interrupted at intervals by innumerable questions—all these are near of kin, in fact belong to the same family, and are represented by one general example, the man whom Shakespeare described as a knave very voluble.[3] Shakespeare's description, however, doesn't go far enough; he is truly very voluble, but his volubility is not the worst part of him; it is bad enough, but what makes him altogether distracting is, that all the while he is pouring forth his volume of words, he keeps your hand in his and imparts to it a continuous jogging motion, as if he were turning the crank of a hand organ, only this time the grinder makes the music while the organ does the listening. And he always seizes you when you are in some especial hurry, as for instance when you want to catch that evening train, or when you are on your way to fill some important engagement. But he never considers that; a more leisurely man than this old family friend you never saw before, and being leisurely himself, he naturally imagines every one else is, so he talks steadily on and not the slightest change in his calm and complacent countenance shows that he takes the least notice of your impatience. Oh, but he is not a tantalizer! If the hand-crusher is dreadful, his long-winded brother is fearful; one inflicts physical torture, the other mental; one would kill outright, the other by degrees.

There is another personage who should be mentioned here— the jocular bore. So closely is related to his long-winded kinsman that he might almost be represented by him; there is, however, a slight difference, viz.: that while the former continues to shake your hand all the while he is talking, the latter only seizes it at first and soon exchanges it for your button-hole; so that you hate to shake hands with him not so much from dislike of his manner of performing that act, as from the knowledge that by doing it you are committing yourself to a long period of weary listening. I suppose that among all the troubles that Shakespeare had the jocular bore was by no means the least; at all events, so one would judge from the following:

> "Sometimes he angers me
> With telling me of the mole warp, and the ant,
> Of the dreamer Merlin, and his prophecies;
> And of the dragon and a finless fish,
> A clip-wing'd griffin, and a moulten raven,
> A couchant lion, and a rampant cat,
> And such a deal of skimble-skamble stuff
> As puts me from my faith. I'll tell you what—
> He held me but last night at least nine hours,

In reckoning up the several devils' names,
That were his lackeys: I cried—humph—and well—go to—
But mark'd him not a word. O he's as tedious
As is a tired horse, a railing wife;
Worse than a smoky house: I had rather live
With cheese and garlic, in a windmill, far,
Than feed on cates and have him talk to me,
In my summer-house in Christendom."[4]

Poor Shakespeare! His experience, doubtless, was hard, but it was one which is common to man. There are few who cannot from a full heart echo his sentiments.

But let me say in passing that this hand-shaking babbler is no *novus homo*; he can boast a pedigree as old as the oldest. Why even in the days of the Caesars his family was well-known, as doubtless it had been for no short while; one has only to read of Horace's account of the man who rushed up to him on the *Via Sacra*, grasped his hand, and then broke forth with his incessant chatter, to be convinced of the truth of this statement.[5] If we can say no other good of this tormentor, we must at least give him credit for his blue blood.

I suppose we shall have to be content with the few individuals already mentioned as representation of class No. 1. There are many more that one would like to speak of—the man with the pump-handle shake, the Uriah Heaps, with their clammy, sepulchral hands, the dainty miss who touches your hand in much the same manner in which she would touch a bug, and a score of others—but space will not permit.[6] It is necessary to hurry on to the consideration of our second class, represented by the man with whom we like to clasp hands.

What definition is to be given of this person? Are there any specific rules to be laid down—as that he must have a pleasant greeting and a warm and hearty hand-shake, not a vice nor a pump-handle motion, nor any such abomination? Perhaps this would help us some. The true definition, however, is a very simple one; let me use Longfellow's words:

"Oh, how good it feels!
The hand of an old friend."[7]

That's it. Leave out the old if you chose; the last is the principal word. The hand of a friend! Oh, there's where the secret lies, as to whether or not we enjoy clasping hands with a person—is he a friend? Not a friend of to-day, who may be a foe to-morrow, nor a friend of prosperity and popularity, but a *true* friend, one of the very few that each man has upon whom he can at all times rely. We strike hands time and again with a multitude of friends so-called without thinking much about them, for they are here now and gone presently; but the 'hand of an old friend'—whether it is one we see every day, or whether we meet after long years of separation—'ah, how good it feels!' Those of us who have had the experience of being in that loneliest of all lonely situations, in a strange city with an empty purse, can well appreciate the truth of the poet's lines. We are not apt to be over critical at such a time; we don't stop to consider whether he belongs to the muscular, pump-handle, or long-winded class. Oh, no, no! In our joy we only think 'how good it feels.' Travelers tell us it is a pleasure to meet in a strange country one who is only their fellow-countryman; aye, doubtless; but if that fellow-countryman is also an old friend, then what must the pleasure be, and what must be their sensations on clasping hands again!

Of all the hand-clasping that we give and take, the great majority are forgotten a moment after; there are some, however, that we remember—remember now, and shall remember hereafter, till memory itself shall be forgotten in the grave. How can you forget the last touch of that kind hand as you stood by the side of your dying father? And oh, that still more sorrowful day when mother, too, was taken to that blest haven 'where the wicked cease from troubling and the weary be at rest.'[8] It was a very bright day, full of warmth and light and sunshine. The flowers smiled, but you didn't see the flowers; the birds were singing, but you didn't hear the birds; all the world seemed joyous and happy, but it awoke no joy in your sorrowful heart. It was a bright day, yet oh, so gloomy! For upstairs, in that room with the close-down curtains, a pale form lay stretched upon the bed—a form very familiar. Dim and unreal sounded the voice of the grave old doctor, telling you she could not live; as in a trance you went up when she sent for you and stood there with the others by her bedside. How thin and shadowy was her hand, as it lay upon her breast! How light it felt when you took it in yours! She couldn't press yours much—she was too weak then—but little as it was you felt that pressure, nor have you ceased to feel it yet. And when, in the calm of the summer twilight, standing beside a turf covered mound, you listen to the moaning of the pines and the sweet, sad voices of the frogs in the marshes, and your thoughts go back over the lapse of years and you sigh

*   *   *   *   *   *

"For the touch of a vanished hand
And the sound of a voice that is still,"[9]

once more in your fancy you stand by that bed of death, once more you fell that frail hand in yours. That is one of the hand-claspings that you will never forget. Aye, and thank God that you will not!

A Slave Hero
The Hampden-Sidney Magazine 12, 3 (December 1894): 85-90.

In a secluded spot among the Blue Ridge mountains, close beside the historic James, there is a lonely mound, beneath which lie the remains of one of Nature's noblemen. No tall and stately shaft lifts its ambitious head to mark the hero's resting place; no costly trophies lie about his tomb; no fretted vaults above his head resound with songs of poet or eulogy of orator. But above his breast the wild brier grows, and the rattlesnake, crawling over his heart, startles the watchful hare; while overhead the eagle wheels his circling flight, or the vulture sails slowly by.

Beside this lowly tomb I stood late one summer's day and "watched the mountains kiss high heaven" and looked out across the misty river, broad and calm, gently gliding at its own sweet will.[10]

"Beautiful was the night. Behind the black wall of the forest,
Tipping its summit with silver, arose the moon. On the river
Fell here and there, through the branches, a tremulous gleam of the moonlight,
Like the sweet thoughts of love on a darkened and devious spirit."[11]

One bright ray, pure and clear, fell on the grave at my feet, and stooping I brushed aside the briars and weeds that had grown up around the head stone and read the simple legend engraven thereon:

IN MEMORY OF
JAMES PADETT,

A colored slave, who lost his life by drowning, in the noble effort to rescue from death some of his fellow-men, during a freshet on James River.

And as I read, the lines of the Elegy ran through my head—

"Full many a gem of purest ray serene,
    The dark unfathom'd caves of ocean bear;
Full many a flower is born to blush unseen,
    And waste its sweetness on the desert air."[12]

—and I thought that here, indeed, was a fit subject for such noble words.

The inscription on that stone was short, simple, modest. Nothing was said there about the fearful dangers of the hour—the black and awful night, the lurid glare of the lightning, the ominous mutterings of thunder, the incessant downpour of the rain, the howling of the wind, the despairing cries of drowning men, and above and through all, the sullen roar of the river, rushing onward, onward, sweeping all in its terrible course. There was no praise of eulogist; no list of battles fought and cities taken: yet truly, never statesman or poet or warrior had graven on his tomb a record of a nobler deed. For love is the greatest thing in the world, and "greater love hath no man than this, that a man lay down his life for his friends."[13]

There was no word there about his life, his character. Why should there be? Perhaps he was trusty, tried and true—a well-raised, honest servant; if he was, then so much the better. Yet why tell the world of that? He was but a slave. Perhaps he was not so good—he may have had many faults; if so, then 'tis better that they should go unmentioned. Forgive and be forgiven; it is but natural for men to err.

Yet, good or bad, whatever his character may have been, it matters little now; for if we believe with Johnson that "he that once is good is ever great," it suffices for us to know of his one great, good action.[14]

How many graves there are like this one, hidden away in the obscure corners of the earth! How many great and heroic deeds lie buried beneath the shifting sands of the desert, the rocks of the mountains, the waves of the restless sea! How truly indeed it has been said, "The world knows nothing of its greatest men."[15] Greatness, true greatness, is not to lead victorious legions, to rule the nations of the world,

"The applause of listening senates to command."[16]

Many great men, it is true, have done these things, and all honor be given them for it. All honor to Leonidas and his Spartan heroes; all honor to the martyrs of the Alamo! Theirs is indeed true greatness. But the world is all too prone to think that these alone are great, too prone to believe that to have a hero you must have the trumpet's blare, the cannon's roar, the the [sic] thousands and ten thousands slain. We are too apt to take mere exhibitions of hardihood and reckless courage for genuine Golden Deeds.

A Golden Deed is not mere hardihood. There was plenty of hardihood in Napoleon when he led his legions over the Alps into snow-bound Russia—anywhere and everywhere—merely to feed his insatiate lust for empire. But his deeds were not golden.

Nor is a Golden Deed the so-called courage that breaks out in reckless bravado. As Charlotte Yonge says, "there must be something more than mere display of fearlessness. Grave and resolute fulfill-ment of duty is required to give it the true weight."[17] Such duty kept the sentinel at his post at the gate of Pompeii, even when the streams of moulten fire poured faster and faster from the volcano, and the air was thick with fiery hail and suffocating dust, and the fleeing, struggling people prayed and besought him to come away; yet still the sentry stood at his post, stern, silent, unflinching, till his limbs were stiff in death; and his bones, in their casing of armor, have remained even till our own time to show how a Roman soldier did his duty.

"The true metal of a Golden Deed is self-devotion.

    * * It is the spirit that gives itself for others—the
temper that, for the sake of religion, of country, of
duty, of kindred, nay of pity even to a stranger, will
dare all things, risk all things, endure all things,
meet death in one moment; or wear life away in
slow, persevering tendance and suffering."[18]

What, then, constitutes a great man? Pope has given us the answer:

    "Who noble ends by noble means obtains
      * * * *   that man is great indeed."[19]

    And we need not go to Senate halls or battle fields to find the
answer to this description; Whittier warns us to

    "Dream not helm and harness
      The sign of valour true;
    Peace hath higher tests of manhood
    Than battle ever knew."[20]

    And certainly his words were rightly spoken. To die on the
battle field, fighting for one's country, where the eye of your leader
may mark your valor and proclaim it to the world; to stand forth before
your fellow-man as the champion of right and justice against the
tyranny of the oppressor—to do any great deed before the eyes of the
world is not so very difficult; for the reward is great—the deed is
known to fame; and in after years histories will be written, monuments raised, poems sung and eulogies spoken about the great deed
and its doer. And if, like Cicero, we live for the future, what greater
reward could we desire?[21] Yes, yes; Fame, though it be "a fancied life
in others' breath," is unwelcome to few, and it is not hard to suffer
with it assured.[22]

    But ah! To spend one's life in faithful performance of duty,
to pour out one's blood for one's fellow-men, and go down to an
obscure grave, unknown, unpraised—this is hard; but this once done,
if done in the right spirit, is the mark of a hero indeed. When, in your
search for a great man, you come upon one who with Pope can say

"One self-approving hour whole years outweighs
Of stupid starers and of loud huzzas,"[23]

and who has learned to "do good by stealth and blush to find it fame,"
then stop; your object is accomplished.[24] You have found one who,
when he comes to die, will have so lived

* * "that Nature may stand up
And say to all the world: This was a man."[25]

But though James Padett be unknown in history; though no
poet may celebrate his deed in flowing verse, yet his memory will not
perish nor the effect of his example be lost, To-day a white stone, plain
but effective, marks the spot, and on it is inscribed in simple language
the record of the deed. While years ago, when boats still ran on the old
canal nearby, doubtless many a wondering passenger was pointed to
the simple head board hard by the lock, while the captain told in few
but earnest words the pathetic story of the slave and his glorious act;
and on many a wintry night, when the snow lay deep and the north
wind blew cold and sharp from the mountains, the "young marsters
and mistesses from the great house" have gone down to the negroes'
quarters, there to sit in the ruddy fire light and listen with wide-open
eyes and excited countenances while some aged "granny" tells how
"Po' Jim got drownded tryin' to save the white folks." And many a
weary wanderer, passing along the railroad that now runs over the old
tow path, has turned aside to spell out the inscription on that head-
stone, has stood and pondered long and looked out toward the horizon
and pondered and looked again where the clouds and the mountains
meet' but he doesn't see the clouds or the mountains—no, he is
looking beyond, far beyond, over the stretch of wasted years, at a
scene that arises before his mind: a picture of a fair young mother, and
by her side a bright-faced, flaxen-haired boy, who is listening with
sparkling eyes and parted lips while the mother tells him stories—
those old, old stories of the heroes; of Leonidas and his Spartan band;
of Horatius, who kept the bridge; of David who slew the giant; and he
sees the boy's face light up with all the animation of his youthful spirit
as he looks up at his mother and asks how soon he will be big enough

to do such glorious things. He recognizes that picture. Ah! yes, that mother's face he can never forget, and the little boy was once himself; and as he looks, a strange feeling comes over him—a feeling like that of the long ago—and he wonders if he may not yet do something great and good to atone for the past. And as he takes up the burden of life once more and walks on down the railroad, perhaps within that rugged breast have been fanned into glowing the long smouldering embers of a better life. Who knows?

And so that lowly grave, out in the mountains though it be, has nevertheless taught many a lesson, sobered many a wayward life, and pointed many to higher and nobler aims.

And still as the seasons come and go, the mountains, grander monuments than ever raised by human hands, lift their hoary summits around the hero's grave, fit emblems of such ennobling deeds; while the river, like the life of every mortal, rushing onward to the great unknown, ever sings for him his appropriate requiem, the song of the true and the brave.

Notes

1. The quotation, "Bid farewell to every fear," is part of a hymn by Sir Isaac Watts; however, the reference to the "old lady in the story" has not been identified. The first verse of the original hymn, untitled, reads,

> "When I can read my title clear
> To mansions in the skies,
> I'll bid farewell to every fear,
> And wipe my weeping eyes."

2. The essay "Bores" was published in *Nineteenth Century* 35 (February 1894): 284-301. It is also included in a collection of essays by Sir Herbert Maxwell: *Post Meridiana: Afternoon Essays* (London: William Blackwood, 1895): 115-145, published one year after Sommerville's article appeared in *The Hampden-Sidney Magazine*.

In his account of the evolution of the Bore since the eighteenth century, the age of the satirists, Maxwell describes the "jocular bore" as one "so fearful in his manifestations as to drive persons to such hazardous means of escape as are resorted to only in moments of extreme terror." (*Post Meridiana*, 125). This kind of person is one who, in spite of his intellectual accomplishments, buttonholes his victims and subjects them to dull stories and "rancid epigrams." Briefly digressing, he remarks, "It is not possible, of course, to compile statistics of the motives actuating the people who are run over and killed each year in Piccadilly, for a man's latest thoughts perish with him; but there is good ground for believing that such accidents are chiefly owing to two causes—drink, and precipitate flight on the approach of a Bore of the kind above described." (126)

3. Iago's description of Cassio in *Othello II*, i, 232-44.

4. *I Henry IV III*, i, 146-162.

5. *Satire 9*: 1-5. Horace writes:

> Ibam forte via sacra, sicut meus est mos,
> Nescio quid meditans nugarum, totus in illis:
> Accurrit quidam notus mihi nomine tantum;
> Arreptaque manu, 'Quid agis, dulcissime rerum?'
> 'Suaviter, ut nunc est,' inquam, '& cupio omnia
> quae vis.'

Perchance I was walking along the Via Sacra, as is my wont, thinking about I don't know what, wholly engrossed in my thoughts: Someone whom I knew only by name ran up and having grasped my hand, said, "How are you, my dearest friend?"

I replied, "Well, thank you, for now, and at your service."

After this exchange of pleasantries Horace is unable to get rid of the man until he is summoned into court. He then coerces the poet to appear as a witness, to which he agrees only to silence the chatterer. As the man is hauled off to court, Horace makes his escape.

6. Uriah Heap, an unctuous character in Charles' Dickens' *David Copperfield*, was forever rubbing his long, clammy hands together as he referred to himself as "very 'umble."

7. Henry Wadsworth Longfellow, *John Endicott* in *New England Tragedies*, (Boston: Ticknor & Fields, 1868): 7-95. See IV, i, p. 66. In this play about the persecution of Quakers in Puritan New England, Simon Kempthorn, a sea-captain, has been put in the stocks for swearing. As he is released when his sentence is completed, Ralph Goldsmith, a fellow sea-captain, comes along and shakes Simon's hand. Sommerville's readers, students who had probably read the same

texts in their literature classes, might well have been in on the joke.

8. The source is probably Job 3:17, which ends in "be at rest": "There the wicked cease from troubling; and there the weary be at rest," but the use of "where" is closer to lines 47-48 in Gerald Massey's poem, "Jerusalem the Golden": "Where the Wicked cease from troubling-/The Weary are at rest!"

9. Alfred, Lord Tennyson, "Break, Break, Break," 11-12. The entire stanza reads:

> And the stately ships go on
>> To their haven under the hill;
> But O for the touch of a vanish'd hand,
>> And for the sound of a voice that is still!

10. Perhaps a reference to Percy Bysshe Shelley, "Love's Philosophy," 8-9:

> See the mountains kiss high heaven,
> And the waves clasp one another;

11. Henry Wadsworth Longfellow, *Evangeline* III, 140-43.

12. Thomas Gray, *Elegy Written in a Country Church-Yard,* 53-56.

13. John 15:13. This quotation from Scripture also appears on the fly-leaf of the 1888 edition of Charlotte Yonge's *Book of Golden Deeds* from which Sommerville quotes below. Thus, he may have had this edition in his possession.

14. Ben Jonson, *The Forest: XIII. Epistle to Katharine, Lady Aubigny,* 52.

15. Henry Taylor, *Philip Van Artvelde I,* v, 19.

16. *Elegy Written in a Country Church-Yard,* 61.

17. *A Book of Golden Deeds of All Times and All Lands Gathered and Narrated by the Author of "The Heir of Redclyffe,"* comp and ed. Charlotte Mary Yonge (London: Macmillan, 1888): 4. Sommerville's editors may have inadvertently placed the first quotation mark after "there." In the original the line reads: "A Golden Deed must be something more than mere display of fearlessness. Grave and resolute fulfillment of duty is required to give it the true weight." The next paragraph of Sommerville's definition of a Golden Deed is a paraphrase of Yonge:

> Such duty kept the sentinel at his post at the gate of Pompeii, even when the stifling dust of ashes came thicker and thicker

from the volcano, and the liquid mud streamed down, and the people fell and struggled on, and still the sentry stood at his post, unflinching, till death had stiffened his limbs; and his bones, in their helmet and breastplate, with the hand still raised to keep the suffocating dust from mouth and nose, have remained till our own times to show how a Roman soldier did his duty. (4)

18. The complete quotation reads: For the true metal of a Golden Deed is self-devotion. Selfishness is the dross and alloy that gives the unsound ring to many an act that has been called glorious. And, on the other hand, it is not only the valour, which meets a thousand enemies upon the battle-field, or scales the walls in a forlorn hope, that is of true gold. It may be, but often it is mere greed of fame, fear of shame, or lust of plunder. No, it is the spirit that gives itself for others—the temper that for the sake of religion, of country, of duty, of kindred, nay of pity even to a stranger, will dare all things, risk all things, endure all things, meet death in one moment, or wear life away in slow, persevering tendance and suffering. (5)

19. Alexander Pope, *Essay on Man, IV*, 233-236:
> Who noble ends by noble means obtains,
> Or failing, smiles in exile or in chains,
> Like good Aurelius let him reign, or bleed
> Like Socrates, that man is great indeed.

20. John Greenleaf Whittier, "The Hero," 73-76.

21. See *On Old Age*, 33.82, where Cicero argues that one purpose for living is to benefit future generations. The soul, being immortal, looks to the future, a source of inspiration in this life and protection from the fear of death.

22. Possibly Alexander Pope, *Temple of Fame*, 505-506:
> How vain that second life in others' breath,
> Th' estate which wits inherit after death!

23. *Essay on Man, IV*, 253-258:
> All fame is foreign but of true desert,
> Plays round the head, but comes not to the heart:
> One self-approving hour whole years out-weighs

Of stupid starers, and of loud huzzas;
And more true joy Marcellus exil'd feels,
Than Caesar with a senate at his heels.

24. Alexander Pope, *Epilogue to the Satires Dialogue 1*, 135-136:

Let humble ALLEN, with an awkward Shame,
Do good by stealth, and blush to find it Fame.

Here Pope is satirizing the gentleman who does good deeds only to spread his own reputation. Thus Sommerville inverts Pope's irony to describe the ideal hero.

25. Mark Antony's eulogy of Brutus in *Julius Caesar V*, v, 74-75.

Bibliography

Adams, George and Melva. Interview with author, June 1983.

Annual Reports of the Executive Committee of Christian Education and Ministerial Relief of the Presbyterian Church in the U.S. Montreat, North Carolina: The Historical Foundation of the Presbyterian and Reformed Churches, Inc., 1936.

Annual Report of the Lynchburg Art Club. Jones Memorial Library. Lynchburg, Virginia.

Argonaut (1942): Dedication Page. Lynchburg College Archives.

Bergson, Henri. *An Introduction to Metaphysics.* Translated by T. E. Holme. New York: G.P. Putnam's Sons, 1912.

—. *Matter and Memory.* New York: The Macmillan Company, 1929.

Blunt, Ruth Homes. *The Lynchburg Art Club and Its Affiliates.* Lynchburg: The Mutual Press.

Brickhouse, Robert L., M.D. Interview by phone with author, 10 June 1987.

Broad, Charles Dunbar. "Introduction." *Scientific Thought.* New York: Harcourt, Brace and Company, 1923.

Brown, Stuart E. Jr. *Annals of Clarke County Virginia Old Homes, Families, Etcetera.* Virginia: The Virginia Book Company, c1983.

Bruchey, Stuart. Interview with author, 7 February 1984.

Bryan, William L. *War of Families of Minds.* London: The Oxford Press, 1940.

The Bulletin of Lynchburg College. Office of the Registrar Publications, 1924-38. RS#37/3/1. Box 1. 1938-48. Box 2. The Lynchburg College Archives.

Cabot, Richard Clarke. *What Men Live By.* Boston and New York: Houghton Mifflin Company, 1929.

Calkins, Mary W. *The Persistent Problems of Philosophy.* New York: Macmillan, 1925.

Catalogue of the Officers and Students of Hampden-Sidney (1891): 1-35; (1895): 6, 33.

The Catalogue. Lewisburg Seminary for Girls 1913-1914. Montreat, North Carolina: The Historic Foundation of the Presbyterian and Reformed Churches, Inc., 1913-1914.

The Catalogue, Hampden-Sidney College 27 (1896): 42-44; (1897): 9.

The Catalogue of Lynchburg College. See *The Bulletin of Lynchburg College.*

Charter Members and Minutes and Annual Meetings, November 1921 to May 1949 (Lynchburg Art Club). Jones Memorial Library.

Confederate Consolidated Index. Washington, D.C.: The National Archives.

Couper, William. *The V.M.I. New Market Cadets Biographical Sketches of all Members of the Virginia Military Institute Corps of Cadets who fought in the Battle of New Market, May 15, 1864.* Virginia: The Michie Company, 1933.

Darst, Jackson. "Behind That Desk - Richard Clarke Sommerville." *The Prism* 7 (1943): 9, 16.

Descartes, Rene. "Meditations on First Philosophy." In *The Philosophical Works of Descartes,* edited by E.S. Haldane. Cambridge: The University Press, 1911-12.

Eastman, Mary. *Dahcohtah; or Life and Legends of the Sioux around Fort Snelling.* Preface by C.M. Kirkland (New York: John Wiley), 1849.

Eby, Amy Bowen. *Amelia of Another Day.* Unpublished, 1984.

—. Letter to Mervyn Williamson, 28 January 1972.

Eddington, A.S. "The Fitzgerald Contraction." and "Relativity." In *Space, Time and Gravitation.* Cambridge: The University Press, 1923.

—. "Man's Place in the Universe." and "The Sidereal Universe." *The Nature of the Physical World.* New York: The Macmillan Company, 1929.

Evans, W. Donald. Interview with author, June 1987.

Evans, Rand B. "The Origins in American Academic Psychology." In

Explorations in the History of Psychology in the United States, edited by Josef Brožek. Lewisburg, Pennsylvania: Bucknell University Press; London and Toronto: Associated University Presses, 1984.

Fauntleroy, A. M. *The Record of Hampden-Sydney Alumni Association 4.* 2 (January 1930): 12.

Flemming, E.G. "The Predictive Value of Certain Tests of Emotional Stability as Applied to College Freshmen." *Archives of Psychology 96* (May 1928).

Freer, Phillips. Letter to author, 10 September 1987.

Greer, Bonnie, Letters to author with enclosures, 25 November 1985.

—. Letter to author, 15 August 1985.

Hailey, Robert. Interview with author, 3 June 1987.

Haldane, J.S. *The Philosophy of a Biologist.* Oxford: The Clarendon Press, 1935.

Helsabeck, Fred, and Weldon Thompson. "Intergroup Relations at Lynchburg College." In *Intergroup Relations in Teacher Education 1*, edited by L.A. Cook. Washington, D.C.: American Council on Education. (1950-51): v-vi, 245-269. 256ff.

Hemphill, Ruby. Letter to author with enclosures, 31 July 1985.

Henderson, A. Reston. Letter to author with enclosures, 24 May 1984.

History of Virginia in Autobiography 5 and 6. Chicago and New York: The American Historical Society, 1924.

Hilgard, Ernest. *Psychology in America, A Historical Survey.* San Diego: Harcourt Brace Jovanovich Publishers, 1987.

Hocking, William E. *The Meaning of God in Human Experience.* New Haven: The Yale University Press, 1912.

—. "Why the Mind Needs a Body." *The Self Its Body and Freedom.* New Haven: The Yale University Press, 1928.

Hopkins, C. H. *History of the Y.M.C.A. in North America.* New York: Associated Press, 1951.

Hothersall, David. *History of Psychology.* New York: Random House, 1984.

224   BIBLIOGRAPHY

Hume, David. *A Treatise on Human Nature.* Oxford: Clarendon Press, 1896.

Hynds, Margaret. Letter to author with summary of newspaper accounts, *The Milford News* (August 26, 1916). 1985.

Intergroup Relations in Teacher Education 1. Ed. L.A. Cook. Washington, D.C.: American Council on Education, 1950-51.

James, William. *Pragmatism.* London: Longmans, Green, 1913.

—. *The Variety of Religious Experience.* New York: The Modern Library, 1936.

Jeans, James. "The Earth." *Through Space and Time.* New York: The Macmillan Company; Cambridge: The University Press, (1934): 1-47.

Jordan, Stanley. Interview with author, 23 March 1983.

Kaleidoscope (1891 through 1896). Hampden-Sydney College Archives.

Kant, Immanuel. "Theory of Ethics." In *Kant Selections.* Edited by Theodore Meyer Greene. New York: Charles Scribner's Sons, c1929

Keeton, Libbie, and Reggie Thomas. "Dr. Richard Clarke Sommerville." *The Prism.* (May 1946): 6-7.

Lemmon, V.G. "The Relation of Reaction Time to Measures of Intelligence, Memory, and Learning." *Archives of Psychology 94* (November 1927).

Lewis, Clarence I. *Mind and the World Order.* New York: Dover Publications, 1929.

Little Theatre Scrap Book 1921-29. Jones Memorial Library.

Lynchburg Art Club Scrapbook 1891-1951. Jones Memorial Library.

Lynchburg Art Club Scrapbook #1 1924-59. Jones Memorial Library.

Marx, Melvin H., and William A. Hillix. *Systems and Theories of Psychology.* 3rd edition. New York: McCraw Hill Book Company, 1979.

McDougall, William. "Emergent Evolution." *Modern Materialism and Emergent Evolution.* New York: Van Nostrand Co., 1929.

McMaster, Richard K. *The History of Hardy County - 1786-1986.*

West Virginia: Walsworth Press, Inc., 1986.

Mervyn Williamson Papers. Lynchburg College Archives.

Minutes, SPECS Club Meetings 1922-1952. Lynchburg College Archives.

Minutes of the Executive Committee of the Board of Trustees. In Trustees, Board, Secretary Meeting Minutes 1909—; Meeting Minutes 1909-1954. RS#1 1/2/1 Box 1. Lynchburg College Archives.

Minutes of the Faculty. In Dean of the College Academic Program Faculty Council Meeting Minutes, Faculty Minutes 1911-1935. RS#1/2/1 Box 1. 1935-1948, Box 2. 1936-1962, Box 3. Lynchburg College Archives.

The Minutes of the Philanthropic Society II, 1885-1891, 9, 19, 21-28, 60, 80, 82, 220. Hampden-Sydney Archives.

Montgomery, Riley B. Letter to Richard Sommerville, 13 March 1945.

—. Letter to Richard Sommerville, 2 April 1948.

—. *Reminiscence of Riley Benjamin Montgomery 1 and 2.* Unpublished, Lynchburg College Archives.

Morgan C. L. "Emergence." *Emergent Evolution.* New York: Henry Holt and Company, 1928.

Morgan, Goodbar. Letter to author with enclosures, 2 June 1983.

Morton, Frederic. *The Story of Winchester in Virginia (1776-1861).* Virginia: Shenandoah Publishing House, 1924.

Morton, Richard L. *Virginia Since 1861* 3 Chicago: The American Historical Society, 1924.

Norment, Meredith, Jr. "An Appreciation" (1964).

Palmer, Paul R. Letter to Carol Pollack, 30 June 1986.

—. Letter to author with enclosures from the *University Bulletin,* 10 July 1986.

Patterson, Donald G. *Physique and Intellect.* New York: The Century Company, 1930.

Paulson, Friedrich. *Introduction to Philosophy.* Henry Holt and Co., 1930.

Payne, Polly. Interview with author, July 1987.

Perry, Ralph B. *Present Philosophical Tendencies*. New York: Longmans, Green and Co., 1938

"Plato - Uranians Hold Annual Banquet." *The Critograph 29* (1943): 7.

Play Bill. "Meet the Cast." *Little Theatre Scrapbook* (1948-53). Jones Memorial Library.

Poffenbarger, A.T. *Applied Psychology, Its Principles and Methods*. New York: D. Appleton and Company, 1928.

Presidential Papers, File 2/8/6, Box 7, Lynchburg College Archives.

Proceedings of the SPECS Club, 1, 1936-1937; 1937-38; 1938-39. RG 40. Lynchburg College Archives.

Proceedings of the SPECS Club, 13 April 1942. Uncatalogued. Lynchburg College Archives

Proceedings of the SPECS Club, 11 January 1944. Uncatalogued. Lynchburg College Archives.

Redd, Virginia and John Brinkley. Interview with author, June 1984.

Robinson, Dale. *The Academies of Virginia (1776-1861)*. Richmond: The Dietz Press, Inc.,1977.

Roster of the Lynchburg Art Club. Jones Memorial Library, Lynchburg, Virginia.

Russell Bertrand. *The ABC of Atoms*. New York: E.P. Dutton and Co., 1923.

—. *Problems of Philosophy* London: The Oxford Press, 1912.

The Savannah Morning News (1900-1911). J. H. Estill Publishers. Microfilm Publications. Rochester, New York: The University of Rochester Library.

Schoenmaker, Yon. "Dr. Richard C. Sommerville Relates Varied Events of Unusual Career." *The Critograph 39* 11 (May 1953): 5.

See, R.G. "The Last Comrade." *The Record of Hampden-Sydney 44 and 45*. (1970-71): 16.

Shackelford, William. Interview with author, 11 March 1983.

Shepardson, F.W. *The Story of Beta Theta Pi.* Wisconsin: The Collegiate Press, George Banta Publishing Co., 1930.

Sommerville, James. *Somerville Family of White Post, Virginia.* Unpublished: Welton Family Papers.

Sommerville, Richard. Letter to Felix and Francis Welton, 17 September, 1948.

—. Letter to President J.T.T. Hundley, 5 March 1934.

—. Letter to Riley B. Montgomery, 4 April 1936.

Sommerville, Richard Clarke. *American Men of Science.* 8th Edition. Ed. Jacques Cattell. Lancaster, Pennsylvania: The Science Press, 1947.

Sommerville, Richard Clarke. "As a Man Thinketh." *The Prism 2* (February 1940): 6-7, 15-16.

—. "Editorial." *The Hampden-Sidney Magazine,* 13 1 (1895): 22, 55.

—. "Editorial." *The Hampden-Sidney Magazine,* 2 (1895): 55.

—. "Faculty Hob-nobs." *The Prism 1* (1939): 5, 7, 16.

—. "The Mesomorphic Revolution." *Minutes of the SPECS Club* (1947).

—. "Oola-Ita." *The Hampden-Sidney Magazine 11,* 6 (March 1894): 310-314.

—. "The Old Timer." *The Moorefield (West Virginia) Examiner* (10 October 1956): 5.

—. "Physical, Motor, and Sensory Traits." *Archives of Psychology 75* (1924): 28.

—. "Some Remarks on Hand-Shaking." *The Hampden-Sidney Magazine 12* 1 (October 1894): 15-20.

—. "The Slave-Hero." *The Hampden-Sidney Magazine 12,* 3 (December 1894): 85-91.

Stanger Allen. Interview with author, 16 April 1983.

Stensland, Anna Lee, and Aune M. Fadum, *Literature by and about the American Indian: An Annotated Bibliography.* 2nd ed. (Urbana: National Council of Teachers of English), 1979.

The Student's Hand-Book #2 10.

Student's Register 1849-1905. Hampden-Sydney Archives.

Sullivan, John William Navin. "The Revolution in Science." *Atlantic Monthly* 151 (1933): 286-94.

Sydnor, Lavelon. Interview with author, 15 March 1983.

Texas Presbyterian College Bulletin. 1916-1917.

Thompson, Ernest T. *History of the Presbyterians in the South, I* Richmond: John Knox Press, 1973.

Thorne, Frederick C. "Reflections on the Golden Age of Columbia Psychology." *Journal of the History of the Behavioral Sciences* 12 (1976): 160.

Van Valen, Leigh. "Brain Size and Intelligence." *The American Journal of Physical Anthropology 40* (1974): 417.

Wake, Orville. "A History of Lynchburg College, 1903-1953." (Ed.D. unpublished diss., University of Virginia, 1957).

—. Letter to Richard Sommerville, 13 September 1949.

Watson. Robert I. *The Great Psychologists.* 4th edition. Philadelphia: J.P. Lippincott Company, 1978.

Watt, John Sinclair. "History of the Philanthropic Society." Unpublished: undated. Hampden-Sydney Archives.

The Welton Family Papers, Black Mountain, North Carolina.

Whitehead, A. N. *Science and the Modern World.* New York: The Macmillan Company, 1925.

Who's Who in American Art. Ed. Alice Coe McGlanflin. Washington, D.C.: The American Federation of Art, 1936-37.

Williamson, Mervyn. "Man of Many Parts." *The Lynchburg College Magazine 19* 3 (Fall 1972): 7-10, 8, 10.

Woodworth, Robert B. *A History of the Presbytery of Winchester (Synod of Virginia 1719-1945).* Staunton, Virginia: The McClure Printing Company, 1947.

Woodworth, Robert S. and Edward Thorndike. "The Influence of Improvement on one Mental Function upon the Efficiency of Other Functions." *Psychological Review 8* (1901): 247.

Woodworth, Robert S. and B.G. Marquis. *Psychology* 4th edition. New York: Henry Holt Company, 1947.

Women's Club of Lynchburg Scrapbook 8. (1946-47). Jones Memorial Library.

Wygale, R.W. Letter to Mervyn Williamson with enclosures, 7 January 1972.

Y.M.C.A. Hand-Book (1894): 8, 44.

Young, Kimball. *Personality and Problems of Adjustment.* New York: F.S. Croft and Company, 1947.

Young, Kimball, N.E. Drought, and J. Bergstresser. *Personality and Problems of Adjustment.* New York: F.S. Croft and Company, 1937.

Younghusband, Francis Edward. "An Explorer's Religion." *Atlantic Monthly 158* (1936): 651.

"Zeno of Elea." *Encyclopedia Britannica. (exact year, not referenced).*

Elza C. Tiner has been an assistant professor in the Department of English and director of the Writing Center at Lynchburg College since 1989. From 1987 to 1989 she taught at New York Institute of Technology, Old Westbury. She completed the Ph.D. and M.A. degrees from the Centre for Medieval Studies, University of Toronto, in 1989 and 1981, respectively; the Licentiate in Mediaeval Studies, Toronto, in 1985; and the B.A. degree in English from Seton Hall University in 1979. Her fields of interest include medieval literature and the traditions of classical rhetoric in education.

For her research on patronage of medieval and Renaissance travelling companies, she was awarded the Mednick Memorial Fellowship from the Virginia Foundation for Independent Colleges in 1990 and a grand from the American Association of University Professors in 1988. She has published biographies of patrons of travelling companies with the Records of Early English Drama, University of Toronto. Other articles include studies of classical and medieval rhetoric in medieval drama, and applications of ancient rhetorical theory to modern composition teaching.

She is a member of the Modern Language Association; National Council of Teachers of English; Virginia Association of Teachers of English; Medieval and Renaissance Drama Society; International Society of the History of Rhetoric; Canadian Society for the History of Rhetoric; and Council of Writing Program Administrators.

INDEX

Peggy A. Pittas has been teaching in the Department of Psychology at Lynchburg College since 1971 where she has served several terms as department chairperson. She is also an associate of the college's Belle Boone Beard Gerontology Center. She received her master's degree in psychology from Dalhousie University in Halifax, Nova Scotia, and a B.A. degree from Bridgewater College in Bridgewater, Virginia. She was employed as a Counselling Psychologist in the Counselling Center at Dalhousie University from 1968-1971. Her fields of interests include the history of psychology, gerontology, and experiential education.

She has previously published short articles on Richard Sommerville and on the history of psychology at Lynchburg College and was a contributor to the <u>Symposium Readings: Classical Selections on Great Issues</u> (10 vol.) University Press of America, Washington, D.C. (1982).

She is a member of the Virginia Psychological Association; Virginia Academy of Sciences; The Gerontological Society of America; Psi Chi National Honor Society; and the American Association of University Professors.